Germany *to* **Georgia**

Ten Generations of an American Family

CHARLES O. SUMMEROUR

Germany to Georgia:
Ten Generations of an American Family

ISBN 978-0-578-95844-6
LCCN 2021919554

Book design by StoriesToTellBooks.com

Germany *to* Georgia

H
Sommerau
34

CONTENTS

Preface

In September of 2019, the Johns Creek (Georgia) Historical Society held a "Family Farm Day" that included families who had owned farms in their newly incorporated city. Since my family had owned several large farms in the area in the 1800s, I was glad to represent several generations of my family. After this meeting, the Historical Society asked me to present a program on my family. I began digging into my large volume of genealogical information, data passed on to me by other family members, and other files on my well-researched family. As I did so I realized that the information needed to be consolidated into a paper or book. My inclination was that it was time to take the volumes of information accumulated since my family arrived in the Colonies in 1748 and expand it to include the 10 generations that followed. I realized there was a family story worth sharing and at the same time fulfill the goal of paying tribute to my family and accurately portraying my ancestors, who had an honorable past and had influenced the growth and development of much of North Georgia. Documenting the many admirable family traits of honesty and caring for family and friends became important motivation for me.

Fortunately, the Summerour genealogy and various parts of its history had often been recorded and, in some cases, published. My challenge soon became organizing my numerous files and doing more research to expand my understanding of our family, which arrived here 28 years before the Declaration of Independence! Knowing that, recounting family history as recorded by kinfolks like Ben F. Summerour, Ethel and Florence Summerour, and Susan Moore Teller added much authenticity to this work. Current-day historians like Joan Compton, president of the Johns Creek (Georgia) Historical Society, provided great research and support to me in this process. You can see more information about these and others in the Acknowledgements section.

My son, Charles "Knox" of Generation 9, used his finely tuned music-composing skills to provided editing and manuscript review. He may tell you that covering his father's ineptitude was more of a challenge than he would have preferred. But much of the credit for the original layout and typing go to him.

Special thanks to my wife, Annette, who always wanted to see me busy and served as my primary sounding board for much of this work. Her patience and understanding in this effort are greatly appreciated. I was blessed to celebrate 50 years with her in February 2021.

CHAPTER 1

Auraria

Generations 3, 4

The fortunes and future of my Summerour family were forever changed when Henry Summerour III (1787–1849) and his sons immersed themselves in the frenzy of America's first large gold rush. Around 1828 a man named Benjamin Parks was out deer hunting in North Georgia when he kicked up a rock that caught his eye. After examining the rock, he later concluded it was indeed gold. Years later, he recalled "such excitement you never saw . . . and within a few days, it was [as] if the whole world had heard of it. For men came from every State I had ever heard of. They came afoot, on horseback, and wagons, acting more like crazy men than anything else." As Parks related, they were soon "panning out of the branches, and making holes in the hillsides,"[1] Thus was born the first large gold rush in the United States. While historians may differ on the origin of the discovery of gold in Georgia, the rush was nevertheless on and would rapidly change a sleepy community almost overnight.

The original name of this area of North Georgia was Dean, after William Dean, who settled there in 1832. It was later named Nuckollsville, after Nathaniel Nuckolls, who was likely the first—but certainly not the only one—to open a tavern, a seemingly necessary business, given the array of those who soon arrived. The name Nuckollsville continued to be used somewhat jokingly, and an associate of John C. Calhoun of South Carolina, who had also come to the area in 1832 to open a mine, suggested another similar name. (Calhoun would later serve as vice president of the United States under John Quincy Adams and Andrew Jackson.) Later, when the Legislature of Georgia established Lumpkin County, the local citizens felt it was time for an official name for their little town. One of the leading local citizens, Major John Powell, suggested "Auraria," meaning "gold mine" or "gold region." Everyone was satisfied.[2] The local newspaper, *The Western Herald,* which commenced publishing in April of 1831, said the town's "locality [sic] entitled it to the name which it bears, being one as we conceive, of melodious sound accompanied with classic taste and appropriate derivation."[3]

The establishment of the area as a mecca for gold was greatly complicated by factors which both hindered and, in some strange ways, aided the growth of gold mining and all that came with it. For many years this area of North Georgia had been claimed as the tribal territory of the massive Cherokee nation. In 1832 the State of Georgia divided the land into several counties, including Carroll, DeKalb, Gwinnett, Hall, and Habersham, an arrangement that was later tweaked—all to displace the Cherokees from what had suddenly become valuable land. In the process the state decided that "all white persons residing among the Cherokees"[4] were subject to the laws of the state, a decision which rankled some leading citizens, particularly, the family of John Rogers, who had married into the Cherokees. This family would later have great influence and involvement regarding the posture and future of their Cherokee kinsman.

Since 1802 the Federal Government and, particularly, the State of Georgia had enacted laws designed to clear the area of Cherokees. In 1832 Georgia instituted the Land Lottery under provisions of a law passed many years earlier that was used to distribute unclaimed land or land controlled by the state. This action initiated a statewide lottery among all citizens who met certain criteria, giving some families the right to make more than one draw. The lottery began in the fall of 1832 and ended in May the following year. Given the fact that the lands in the lottery may very well have included gold-rich areas, there was naturally a scramble for it, which resulted in mass confusion, fraud, and questions of true ownership. Since mining was already underway in much of the surrounding area, miners were often found working on land they either did not own or for which they could not prove ownership. In some measure, and for a length of time, possession took precedence, as some land was already producing gold. Many residents in the gold mining area were indignant toward the State of Georgia. Thus, the state had carved a deep divide in the minds of both white residents *and* the Cherokees.

In the middle of these tumultuous but vibrant times stepped the Summerour family, who established their roots in Auraria around 1832. Henry Summerour III (1748–1849) had moved to the tiny town of Between, Georgia, in Walton County, about 1827, where he joined his brother, John Summerour Sr. (1792–1867). In the move to the heart of gold country, he brought with him his wife, Sarah Salome Seitz (1790–1843), and his three sons: Harrison, born in 1814 in North Carolina; Benjamin Franklin, born 1817 in North Carolina; and John Lafayette, born in 1827 in Walton County. Although little is known about them, genealogical records show a son Michael Dekalb (b.18190 and daughters, Anna Maria (b.1819) and Susannah (b. 1823). On reaching Auraria to became one of 15 to 20 merchants who supplied the needs of the estimated 1,000 locals and 10,000 area residents who came from all points near and far in pursuit of gold riches. Henry purchased a lot for his store next to the Methodist church, and as an indication of his business acumen, he acquired some gold lots as well. This made him and his family true gold miners, a vocation they would continue for many years.

His initial source of funds for the move to Georgia most likely came from his mother's (Elizabeth Weidner) side. She descended from Henry Weidner, one of the true pioneers of North Carolina, who will be detailed later. It is likely that the two older boys, Harrison and Benjamin Franklin, soon became active with their father, Henry, in the store, and although there is little direct knowledge of its operation, the store likely mirrored many of the others in the town.

In *AURARIA*, the most authoritative book written about this period, E. Merton Coulter provides some intricate details of the store operators of the time. Most of this information is gleaned from *The Western Herald*, a newspaper which, although only in publication from 1831-1832, provides much of what we know about this slice of history. In his chapter on "Merchants, Bankers, Lawyers, Barbers, Doctors in Auraria," Coulter reveals many details about the stores there. And although no direct mention is made of a Summerour store, his stories about a few of the others provide great insight into the types of stores in existence and the merchandise they supplied. Coulter often quotes a writer known as "Billy the Poet," who had this to say about the merchants:

I spoke you'se oftentimes been told
That this here country Is mad [sic] of gold,
But there again we have clever fellows
As Doctors, Lawyers, and Gold Sellers,
The Doctors Scare Lawyers plenty.
I reckon we have nearly twenty.
And Merchants too save each penny
I could not count them, there's so many.

In his book Coulter highlights several merchants who were typical of those who came to serve the needs of the booming area. One local, Major Powell—who had helped choose the name of Auraria—established John M. Powell and Co., which carried groceries sold for "very low prices for Cash only." Perhaps a victim of his own success, he later quit selling groceries. Another merchant, known as "M'Laughlin and Company," claimed to have over $4,000 of dry goods and merchandise ($120,000 in 2020 dollars). S.T. Rowland's store probably qualified as a true department store, as he promoted merchandise brought in from New York and Charleston: "Hammers, Knives, Waffle Irons, Grid Irons, Pad locks, and Knives, Razors, Spades and Shovels." Agricultural products including vegetables, meat, and pork were in such demand that they essentially created a local market. "The infancy of the country and the subsequent scarcity of provisions affords inducements to the agriculturalist of the adjoining counties to look to this market for their surplus products," wrote Coulter.

Corn – 75 to 85 ½ cents per bushel
Meal – 87 ½ cents to $ 1.00 per bushel
Fødder – $2.50 to $3.00 per 100 pounds
Fluor (sic) – $10.00 per barrel
Butter – 18 ½ to 25 cents per pound
Checkens [sic] *– 12 ½ to 18 ¾ cents per pound*
Vegetables – "In Proportion"
Board – $12.00 to 15.00 per month for man
Horse – $10.00 to 12.00 per month

Sales in this unusual market were generally made in cash—although gold was also often used as a method of exchange. This created monetary issues in that there was no uniform weight for, say, a bar of gold. In addition, there was always the debate over the value of gold in its many forms. Even though gold coins had become common, their issuers were always at question. For instance, it was not illegal for a private citizen to issue coins with his own design—a stamp denoting his name and the coin's value—because even though Congress had given this right to the federal government, individuals like Templeton Reed, who operated in the Auraria market, produced coins that could be worth more than their face value. To rectify this momentary dilemma, a new profession was birthed that required someone familiar with the purity and assaying qualities of gold. Residents and miners were finally rewarded for their faith in and patience with the government when, in 1837, a mint was established in Dahlonega, Georgia, just five miles north of Auraria.

Harrison Summerour (1814–1888) was a teenager when he moved to Auraria and began helping his father in the store, observing the new arrivals who both mined and lived there. Family sources mention that he would sometimes go with his father by wagon to Augusta to pick up supplies and merchandise for the store. One family story mentions that he learned "to pick the pockets of the miners"—a joking reference to his budding sense of business, which became more obvious as he grew. Over time we begin to see Harrison's true character exhibited in both commercial and family matters, revealing someone who was honest and loyal to all around him.

In 1839 Harrison married Lucinda Withrow, a marriage that ended after she was found to be unfaithful to him. He decided to divorce her, but when he did, he took great efforts to take care of her, despite her conduct. He made the quite unusual move of hiring an attorney for her to be sure that she was well taken care of in the settlement. Following the divorce, Harrison turned to alcohol to cope with the situation, which did not go unnoticed by those around him. Sometime later, two of his family friends were talking in the store; one was heard to say, "You know, it looks like this thing is going to run Harrison to the dogs." Apparently, when he heard this comment, Harrison "made an about face in this life . . . and regained his former stature."[5]

In 1849 Harrison married Mary Ann Henderson (1928–1911), who came from a prominent family in Forsyth County, Georgia. Sometime after his second wedding, an unkempt, sickly, elderly-appearing woman came to his store. He did not recognize her until she revealed herself as his first wife, Lucinda. She said, "Mr. Summerour, the doctor tells me that I will soon die with consumption (tuberculosis), and before I die, I wanted to come to see you and tell you that you are the finest man I ever knew." Harrison gave her some provisions and she went on her way. This story was told in about 1913 to Ben Summerour by his uncle John Hallman, who years earlier had married Isabella Henderson, a younger sister to Mary Ann, Ben's grandmother.[6]

With the discovery of gold in California in 1849, Aurania's prime years were behind it. But Auraria did not end suddenly; rather, its end came gradually as miners from all over the world flocked to the Golden State. As Coulter writes in the final chapter of his book, "Auraria was a phenomenon. Excitement had produced it and excitement was to end it." As men by the thousands went west, the population of Auraria declined significantly—a Southern business journal listed just five stores and a postmaster in 1854—but gold mining in some form would continue there for decades to come.

Nonetheless, the Summerour family's involvement in gold and gold mining certainly did not end there. When the California Gold Rush began around 1849, the Summerour brothers were still rather young men. Harrison was 35, Frank was 32, and the youngest brother, John L., was only 22. When the two younger brothers decided to try their hand in the new gold country, Harrison "grubstaked," or advanced them the funds to do so, with the provision that they would split the proceeds equally upon their return. While this part of the story, including their return, is well-chronicled in family lore, until recently no details of their actual mining operations in California were known. Thanks to my friend, distant cousin, and family historian extraordinaire, Susan Moore Teller, I am able to share the following, which helps fill in the gaps.

Even getting to California was quite dangerous. A news item from 1852 said that 30 men—five of them from

Lumpkin County—died in a boating accident in Panama while en route to the California gold fields. But the Summerour brothers were both well-equipped—via their mining experience in Lumpkin County—and well-financed, thanks to their older brother Harrison, who likely stayed with his store in Georgia and continued to dabble in goldmining. It appears that John L. and Frank went to California around 1850 and set up mining in Auburn near Sacramento. Thanks again to Susan Moore Teller—who has visited the area and wrote about it in her book *Eliza*—I came upon the following letter, which she shares in her book, and which for the first time gives us a glimpse into the mining adventure of John and Frank. This letter was penned by John L. Summerour.

> *Sluce E. American River California*
> *July 20, 1851*
>
> *Dear Father,*
>
> *It is with much pleasure that I this evening commence dictating a few lines to you. I received your letter of the 24th and content carefully read. It affords much satisfaction to hear from my friends from whom I am so far separated. You have no idea how much joy it affords us poor wonders (wanderers) to hear from home, it gives new life and stirs us up to double our energies to obtain a sufficiency to allow us to go home. Home sweet home is continually ringing in our ears. I have good news to communicate. I am making money as fast as I want it. We made 7 pounds or 1600 dwts (dram weights) in one day. That was yesterday and Thursday 1400 dwts.*

(fn 2) This week 8 hands made 6352 dwts 'side shares which you will see leaves me over 1000 dwts. Me and brother Frank have hands we give them five dollars per diem and board then which makes about six dollars. It is a large price, but we are making a large profit on them. My individual expense is something over fitty dollars for which we have been doing well for 6 weeks past and the profit is as good as ever. I made in that length of time 2300 dwts to 3000. I confidently calculate on making 7000 dwts by the time I go home which will be a handsome sum to start home with.

Perhaps you would like to know about the gold mine we have. I made the discovery myself. It is evidently the bed of some river which has for many ages run here, but it is many hundred feet below this spot. I believe that the north course of the American River had its course here. If you will signal your mind to lead you to the White Path Gold Mine and mark the place where Chastain did so remarkably well, you will have to your view just such a mine as ours with the exception that our mine contains a heavy formation of river gravel and the gold very fine fish scales; it is so abundant we can see it in the dirt. We have panned out as much as 160 dwts at one pan. We have to run our dirt down a shoot some hundred yards, but have surveyed a ditch 1 & ¼ miles long which will bring the water to top of the hills. But we will have to wait for the rains which will be 3 months. It thundered and rained a few drops last night, which is an uncommon thing here; it made me Cthink of home. I had a spell of sickness which lasted about 3 weeks. I was not confined to my bed any of the time, it was cold. Bro. Frank and several have had the complaints, but we are all well now.

The health of the country is very good. The Georgians are doing well as far as I know.

Company that I am connected with is Silas Worley, Tony Thornton, Frank O'Conner and Abram Whitener, (fn 3) we get along first rate. You must know that everyone doesn't agree here even if they C come from the same place. There are many things that would interest you relative to this country. I must inform you that I live in the Devil's Canyon, happily for us the old man has been absent ever since we have bin [sic]here, many remain so Amen. You requested me to write you relative to some report concerning John. I can just say to you that the report is the same is generally two thirds lies. John has enemies in this country, heed not what you hear...

Say to Alexander for me to dismiss forever from his mind any idea of coming to California. Tell him that he can enjoy himself more one day with his family than he could here in 12 months. If he could make a pound a day, I hope I shall never meet any of my cousins here, there is plenty of gold, but the risk is too great.

Do the best you can for my little family while I am absent, and I will numerate (sic)you for your kindness when I return. I hope I am in yours and the families' daily prayers, my friends as well as my enemies and daily before our makers throne.

I need not request any more. I will try the 15th of December to be ready to part for home. You must write me on the receipt of this. Give my love to all you and family. My love to my family through this. Bro. Frank sends his love to. Frank says to Amelda to squeeze little Frank for him. Kiss him for me. This letter must answer for you all, write me often.

Yours with affection and esteem,
John L. Summerour

Mail to: Mr. John Spriggs
Postmaster
Highballs Post Office
Lumpkin County, Ga.

John was writing to his father-in-law John Spriggs, as his own father, Henry Summerour III, had passed away in 1849. Amelda Spriggs is the wife of John Spriggs, thereby the mother-in-law of John L. Abram Whitener is a cousin of John L., as they are both descendants of the pioneer Henry Weidner (see Chapter 2), whose daughter Elizabeth married Henry Summerour II.

Shortly after writing his letter from California, John L. returned to Georgia, probably on horseback or by horse and wagon. We do know that he brought with him a leather satchel containing 14,000 dwts of gold, valued at $7,800 in 1853, which is 786 ounces, valued at $ 1,440,00 in 2021. This story is one of the most oft-related stories in our family history, and the leather satchel was passed down to later generations as a reminder of their family's ties to the California Gold Rush and its impact on the fortunes of the Summerour family.

As the youngest child, John L. remained in mining for many years. He later owned mines in Forsyth and Gwinnett counties, and a mine near his property in Dawson County, near Amicalola Falls. He also joined with his father-in-law, John Spriggs, in numerous mining operations which were probably likened to California-style mining. This method employed diverting water to power a nozzle which blasted soil from the riverbanks where gold deposits were found. One of the Spriggs descendants, Ken Spriggs, described the "Sixty Mine" as being built by the Spriggs-Summerour partnership. He wrote that they took water from the Amicalola River and diverted it along a 19-mile ditch to power their nozzle.

In 1856 John L. Summerour and Ezekiel and Zion Spriggs incorporated the Georgia Water Pan Gold and Copper Company in Gilmer County. Capital was set at $50,000 to $1 Million. Such companies were formed by legislative act, which in this case gave them the right to "locate and construct, through or over any vacant land within the county not represented by legal owner, their main canal, ditch, flume, truss work, or aqueduct, by diverting the streams of named creek."

A group from Kentucky ventured into the Dawson County area in 1881 and bought 640 acres, forming the Kia Mori Mining Company. Again, using hydraulic mining techniques, they needed to divert water from Nibblewill Creek in Lumpkin County by cutting a ditch 33 miles long, 6 feet wide at the top, and 2 feet wide at the bottom. It appears that John L. Summerour did the layout for the ditch. This no doubt was cutting-edge technology for its time. Despite their noble efforts, the Kia Mori mine only operated from 1883 to 1888.[7]

John L. clearly passed on his gold-mining expertise to his family; his grandson David Allen Summerour (1869–1968), known as "Uncle Dave," was such a well-known miner that he has a statue in the Dahlonega Gold Museum in the historic Lumpkin County Courthouse. His obituary notes that he once said, "There's gold still here. When we walked out there was gold just laying [sic] there waiting to be picked up."[8] Uncle Dave worked at the Battle Branch Mine until it closed in the 1930s. He left a large family, as he had 19 children (11 living at his death), 56 grandchildren, and 65 great-grandchildren. Many Summerour descendants of this line populate much of Northern Georgia, North Carolina, and beyond.

While not highlighted in Summerour family history to a large degree, the Civil War obviously impacted them as some—like Frank and Harrison did serve during the war. One incident documented by a letter which references the time just prior to the beginning days of the war tells us a little about their thoughts in that pivotal time in history. For certain the Civil War affected the future well-being of the Summerour family as well as their friends and neighbors,as well be obvious in the following chapters.

Family records also show a letter from John L. Summerour to Amelda Spriggs, his mother-in-law, on December 8, 1860, from Milledgeville, Georgia, the capital of Georgia at the time, when John was there for a

Senate session. The letter seems to indicate he might be a senator, but there is no record of him having been in office. The following excerpts were provided by Susan Moore Teller as she recorded information from Rebekah Slayton Wilson, another family historian. John first writes of his love for Amelda, their family, and his faith in God: "Our heavenly Father has blessed us in the past, and I have faith to believe that he will bless us in the future. That we will be a happy family, and moreover that we will be a God fearing, and useful family in our Country in our day and time."

Later in the letter he writes, "You state to me that the people are somewhat excited about the dissolution of the Union. Well, my dear, if you were here to witness the military parades and to see wagon load after wagon load of guns coming in every day you would think there was excitement in the country. You write to me that you had rather be dead than see this war and hope it to be in our time, and I hope, my dear, that will never happen. We must pray to the Lord, my dear, to help our distracted Nation. We have prayers every morning in the Senate."

In his last paragraph John says, "Don't think we will get away from here short of the end of 4 days. I think we will then adjourn." He then mentions two of his sons: Frank, who was about 11, and Iverson, who was one. "Tell Frank I was very happy in receiving his letter . . . . I will bring him a gun as we will soon be done I must close. Kiss the kids for me. As to little Iverson, God bless him, eat him nearly up but save some for me . . ."[9]

On January 19, 1861, just 49 days after the above letter was written, delegates who were elected on January 1, 1861, adopted the Ordinance of Secession, becoming the fifth state to secede from the Union.

After returning from California, Frank moved to Murray County, Georgia, where he became a leading citizen and established Summerour Methodist Church in Crandall, near Chatsworth. On May 11, 1860, he was appointed U.S. Postmaster in Fancy Hill, Murray County. He fought with numerous units during the Civil War and affirmed his oath to the United States on October 22, 1865, as noted in the U.S. Pardons and Amnesty Proclamation after submitting a request for pardon, as was required.[10,11]

In 1850, with his two brothers still mining out West, Harrison moved his family to another mining area on the Etowah River in Forsyth County, Georgia, where he opened a store in the town known as Hightower, or "Frogtown." He continued his involvement in gold mining there, thus putting his share of the profits gained from the brothers to good use.

John L., Harrison and Frank are said to have loaned Dawson County the money to build the courthouse there, and they also supervised its construction. John L. was said to have written a diary from age 30, kept in a bank vault in Dawsonville. When he passed away in 1887, he was living in a two-story home on Highway 52 in Dawson County, near Amicalola Falls, a house he had purchased after returning home from California. He is buried in the Spriggs-Summerour family cemetery nearby. Unfortunately, to my knowledge, no record of the diary exists today.

From almost any perspective, the fortunes and successes of these brothers would have lasting impact on the future generations of the Summerour family. At the same time, there conscious use of their wealth would set a high standard for their civic and personal conduct.

Auraria 2021. Inscription on the Auraria Historical Marker:

Auraria, (Gold). In 1832 the scene of Georgia's first gold rush, was named by John C. Calhoun, owner of a nearby mine worked by Calhoun slaves. Auraria and Dahlonega were the two real gold towns in the U.S. before 1849. Between 1832 and 1839 about $20,000,000 in gold was mined in Georgia's Cherokee County. From Auraria in 1858,the "Russell boys" led by Green Russell went west and established another Auraria near the mouth of Cherry Creek that later became Denver, Col. Green Russell uncovered a fabulous lode called Russell Gulch near which was built Central City, Col. "Richest square mile on earth."

Harrison Summerour

John L. Summerour

John L's satchel

Uncle Dave Summerour

CHAPTER 2

Sommerau – Summerow – Sumerow

Summerour

Generations 1, 2

One of the questions that seems to have been overlooked in our family's understanding of our immigrant ancestors is why young adults like Heinrich, Johannes, and Susannah would risk leaving Germany to build a new life in an undeveloped British colony. To begin to answer this question, we should first look at the homeland they left and the history of German migration, as well as my forebears' landing in Philadelphia and eventual settling in pioneer North Carolina many years before they came to Georgia.

The homeland of my German ancestors was the area of southwest Germany known as the Palatinate, which was a section of the country left over from the political structure of the Holy Roman Empire. According to *Wikipedia,* Sommerau is a municipality in the Trier-Saarburg District in Rhineland-Palatinate consisting of a 0.4-square-mile area with a current population of only 75.[12] Most of our family history places them in this small village, which has oft been visited by various family members over the years—all of whom reported they found no current Sommerau family residents present. Some have reported there were several other villages with the same or similar name in Germany, but for now we will leave that for others to research.

While their reasons for leaving Germany seem to have been many, most perceive it as being about religious persecution. While this contains an element of truth—most of the immigrants were affiliated with the quite-conservative Lutheran Reformed churches and had found it quite difficult to practice their faith there— "[t]hey left primarily because of the Thirty Years War (1616–1648) and the subsequent war between the German principalities and France."[13] The reference to this period coincides with the immigration of the Sommerau family, which occurred in 1748, as described later. German immigrants seem to have come in family units, although not necessarily all at the same time. They consisted mostly of artisans and tradesmen. One historian describes the typical German immigrant as a poor farmer who arrived around 1750 with a wife and two children. They were mostly in debt for the passage across the Atlantic but had family or friends already settled in America. They were affiliated with the Lutheran or Reformed churches but only loosely committed to an organized religion. Records show they became prosperous members of the community. However, many were too poor to pay the transatlantic passage, so as many as one half to two thirds of the German immigrants came to Pennsylvania as indentured servants, or redemptioners, as Germans called them."[14]

While we do not have many specific details about the Sommerau immigrants, they came to the Colonies as young adults, and in some ways were probably typical of those described. We know they were not married, but as shown later, they married soon after arriving—which likely is an indication that much of their journey was determined prior to leaving their homeland.

German immigration to America had both pull and push elements, with the push being the years of war involving their towns and villages. At the same time, the allure of new land drew the interest of many Germans, who would eventually immigrate to the Colonies. This pull element included the fact that William Penn marketed his new land, its agricultural abundance, its tolerance of religious differences, and his own political views.[15]

German immigration to England by the 1730s, amounting to about 13,000 people, had failed when they could not be absorbed into the already populated area of their adopted country. Thus, the Germans focused on the British colony of Pennsylvania in America, which, by the time of the American Revolution, would see 150,000 to 170,000 immigrants arrive on its shores, approximately one third of them settling around Philadelphia.

Against this backdrop appeared the three first immigrants of the Sommerau/Summerour family. After leaving Rotterdam, Holland, with a stop in Cowes, England, the ship *Patience*, with Captain John Brown and a group of German families, arrived in Philadelphia on September 16, 1748. Included were brothers Henrich, age 27, Johan (age unknown), and sister Susannah (age unknown). Note that women were not listed on the ship's records. After taking the oath and leaving the embarkation center, the three siblings initially joined a group of other German immigrant families near Philadelphia. Putting the time into historical perspective, the oath they took was to the British crown, as this was 28 years prior to the Declaration of Independence. On October 27, 1748, just one month after arriving, Susannah (Susan) married Ulrich Yakely, another immigrant from Saxony. They seemed to have settled in the area around Philadelphia.

Johann (John) also married and later settled on a 100-acre farm in Wyoming Valley, Pennsylvania. While our dedicated family genealogists and historians continue to track down information on Susan and John, we will now focus on my direct ancestor, Heinrich (Henry), who married Mary (surname not known) on December 17, 1748. It is not known if they had become acquainted earlier or met in the group of their kinsmen. They obviously continued their close relationship with the group of 25 or 30 other German families, which is a story we will follow later in detail.

As Germans continued to flock to the Pennsylvania countryside by the thousands, the inhabitants soon found themselves somewhat disadvantaged as land became more costly to acquire. "But the only result of the influx was an agreeable one to property owners as the soil greatly increased in value compelling newcomers to look elsewhere for cheaper land."[16] In addition to property concerns, weather factors also drove some to look elsewhere as they looked for a more moderate climate, along with cheaper land.

One of the areas chosen by some early German immigrants was the Appalachian area of western North Carolina where some had already staked out a new beginning. Here they found cheaper land and both summers and winters that were conducive to farming. The Germans found that North Carolina provided a "kind of middle ground where the staples of the North and South meet in the same fields and flourish in social proximity. It is obvious that the fertility of the soil, the healthfulness of the climate, and the abundance of cheap and unappropriated land were powerful inducements in drawing a large influx of immigrants."[17]

One who had eyed this pioneer territory was a fellow Saxon, Henry Weidner, who would become renowned as one of the first European settlers in western North Carolina and a great supporter of the American Revolution. Shortly after arriving in Philadelphia, Henry and Mary Summerour, along with 25 to 30 other German families led by Weidner, made the long trek to the area of what is now Catawba and Lincoln counties in North Carolina. Weidner and his wife had earlier found the area to be attractive but had to first survive conflict with the native Cherokee and Catawba Indians who lived in the area. After an attack by the Cherokees in which they killed Weidner's sister, brother-in-law, and their children, the early group relocated to South Carolina for two years. Living there, they allowed the Indian uprising to dissipate, and, as intended, then returned to the beautiful Catawba Valley of North Carolina, which is where Weidner eventually led them. Henry Weidner's impact on these German families will be shown later, but his influence on the Summerour family was already evident. On October 6, 1827, Weidner's daughter Elizabeth (1764–1827) married Henry Summerour II (1759–1836), son of Henry and Mary, and much of the livelihood of future Summerour generations would be positively affected by this relationship.

An intriguing aspect of any immigrant family is the transliteration or "Anglicizing" of the name, which in the case of my ancestors is a long-running and still-deliberated issue. Most likely, the German "Sommerau" or "Somerower," both of which appear on the passenger list of the *Patience*,[18] were transliterated (Anglicized) by the British authorities to "Summerour," as that is the name that Henry I used throughout his life, including in the inscription (Heirich) on his tombstone.

That, however, did not seem to prohibit other family members from making their own determinations as to the spelling, as evinced in numerous future generations. In 1996 I visited the burial place of Henry and his sons, Henry II and Michael, and their spouses in the Old White

Church Cemetery, the oldest burial ground in Lincolnton, the town in North Carolina which they eventually called home. This cemetery contains many of the oldest graves in the area and was added to the National Registry of Historic Places in 1994. This visit was for me a solemn time to reflect and remember my ancestors from almost two centuries before. From there we drove to the Saint Matthews United Church of Christ Cemetery on U.S. 321 just outside Lincolnton. The original church was a German Reform Lutheran Church and, evidently, was the home church for later generations of Summerours. Here exist about 75 family graves, which include three different spellings of the family name. One marker is that of Jacob "Tapster" Summerrow, son of Henry II and his wife, Elizabeth Weidner. Other spellings engraved on various markers are "Sumerow" and "Summrow." This was quite intriguing to someone who up until that point had only known the "Summerour" spelling. Over the years many researchers have no doubt stumbled while trying to sort out the various derivations. Susan Moore Teller related how she had to overcome such an obstacle as she was researching our common ancestor, Henry Summerour III: through her analysis of a document granting land to veterans of the Revolutionary War, she was able to prove Henry III a new patriot, for which she earned a blue ribbon on her Daughters of the American Revolution certificate. She was able to match him despite his name being spelled "Sumro," which is probably not unusual for Colonial days, as many family names were spelled phonetically by those of differing languages. For now I will stop here, but suffice it to say there are thousands of relatives of ours who, though they may spell their names differently, would, through modern DNA testing, be able to trace their heritage—as I have done!—to prove they are indeed descendants of Heinrich and Mary Summerour.

Much of what we know about this time in our family's pioneer history comes from the well-known article, "A Celebration of the Germans in North Carolina for 150 years: A Memorial to Old Father Henry Weidner."[19] This commentary appeared in the newspaper *The Newton Enterprise* and records several addresses—including sermons—which were given on a day where all the families in the area, including many ancestors of Henry Weidner, gathered at the old Weidner homestead on May 30, 1894. The various speeches tell us a great deal about the man Henry Weidner, the lifestyle of the people he led, and the example he set for his kinsmen.

Here are some very revealing excerpts from the article:

A Celebration of the Germans in North Carolina for 150 years

A Memorial to the Old Father Henry Weidner

Wednesday morning May 30th dawned upon us dark and gloomy, the heavy clouds hung low, and threatened each moment to deluge the earth with rain, but nothing daunted large numbers of persons [who] were easily seen wandering their way to the hospitable home of John W. Robinson to attend the memorial service to be held that day in honor of Henry Weidner, the discoverer of South Fork, and earliest settler of that part of Catawba County.

On nearing the home of our friend, Mr. Robinson was to be seen standing in his front yard bidding a hearty welcome to each and every visitor as they passed by him, be they in buggy, carriage, wagon, cart, on horseback or on foot. A nice platform had been erected beneath the out-stretching branches of the giant oak tree, which was borne upon its bark the red paint that was the Indian's signal to Henry Weidner and his noble comrades that hostilities had commenced and the trunk of the mighty white oak as well as the speakers platform had been prettily decorated for the occasion.

At 10:30 the chorus of Bethel and Zion gave the audience some very appropriate music and Reve. Mr. Murphy, who was the master of ceremonies, announced the invocation by Rev. A. H. Smith, following with the scripture lessons. Following the prayer, the chorus sang "All Hail the Power of Jesus Name." Mr. John W. Robinson was then introduced who delivered the address of welcome.

John W. Robinson's address:

> *Ladies and gentlemen, I am truly thankful that I have been permitted to see this day on which the descendants and friends of Henry Weidner have assembled under this historic old tree, which stands as a living monument to his memory, to honor the pioneer of the south Fork Valley. Nearby, now in ruins is the home and yonder hill is the resting place of the first white man who saw the beautiful valley of Henry's and Jacob's Forks of the South Fork of the Catawba River. And to you the living relatives of Old Father Weidner, to you kind pastors, and your people, to your neighbors and friends, to all, I on behalf of my family and self, extend a cordial welcome to my home – once the home of Father Weidner.*
>
> *This memorial service was mostly gotten up for your benefit and I congratulate you for having such a brave and great man as Henry Weidner, your ancestor. I trust you will keep this grade. Soon our race will be run, and with what history may be handed down to you today, I trust you will pass it on to your children and grandchildren. I give my thanks for all involved in this occasion.*

At the conclusion of Mr. Robinson's address, Rev. Mr. Murphy arose and said:

> *Mr. Robins, on behalf of all this large assemblage of people, the descendants and friends of Henry Weidner, I sincerely thank you. There is no better way of impressing the important lessons of life upon the minds of our young people than by pointing them to the noble deeds*

of their ancestors.

A certain Latin writer has said that whenever he beheld the images of his ancestors, he felt his mind vehemently exceed to virtue. It was not the wax or marble that possessed and inspired this power, but the recollections of their noble actions, which kindled this generous flame in his bosom. The learned apostle, when he would arouse the Hebrew Christians and inspire them to noble deeds and grater (sic) and truer reverence, released the lives of the heroes of faith who subdued kingdoms and wrought righteousness. We feel that today will gather fresh inspiration, which will enable us to go to higher attainments and greater perfecton in life, Again, we sincerely thank you.

Writer's note: At this point an hour and half was taken for lunch and a time to visit the grave of Henry Weidner.

The introduction was given to Judge Matthew L. McCorkle of Newton. Following is Colonel McCorkle's speech:

It has been customary among all civilized people since the world was created to build monuments to perpetuate the memories of the noble dead and celebrate events in world history.

It has been over one hundred and fifty years since Henry Weidner first discovered yon beautiful river, the South Fork of the Catawba River. When he came here there were no Europeans living along the river. When he crossed the Catawba River at Sherill's Fork, he crossed the boundary of the Indians. From Adam Sherill's Fork, about the year 1845, he started wet without a human soul to pilot him or to accompany him in this unknown land with a gun whose barrel was about six feet long, with a tomahawk, a big knife in his scabbard.

Due West from Sherrill's Fork carried him to where the two rivers of the south Fork came together. He stood on a hill not far from Ilkanah Hutscker's and viewed the landscape o'er. Moses himself was not more delighted to view the land of Cannan. Nightfall overtook him; he laid himself down to sleep with his watch dogs beside him, and his Heavenly Father to guard him from the dangers of the night. One of the beautiful rivers is named Henry and the other Jacob, after Henry and Jacob Weidner.

Henry Weidner was a bold and daring adventurer He originally came from Germany . . . . and if Henry's story is accurate, he was a member of the House of Wetin, Coburg branch. He as Saxon from Coburg, Saxony, and left that country when he was a young man, on account of some trouble between him and his brothers about the Crown government and came to America.

He landed first in Philadelphia, then he came to North Carolina. He was want to go back to the civilized world each spring . . . and on one of his trips he brought back a young wife, Catherine Mull, and a youth by the name of Conrad Yoder . . . and Abram Mull who married Mary Poff. They had not been in the forest long when a band of marauding Cherokees invaded and killed Abraham Mull and two of his children, scalped them and burned their home. Because of this Mrs. Mull, Henry Weidner and his family left for South Carolina, where they lived for about two years, and they all returned to their homes, and were never afterwards molested on account of the Indians.

After Henry Weidner led the way, he was followed by the Holes, Conrads, Reinharts, Anthonys, Frys, Formeys, Rachs, Ramseurs, Doyles, Bosts, Shufords, Summerows, Dellingers, Signmons, and a number of other families, who take them all in all, are a noble set of people. They built their homes over springs and in case of siege of the Indians, they could have water to drink with loopholes in the rock walls from which to shoot their assailants. There is an evidence of the fact in the old dwelling house of Henry Weidner. They carried their lives in their own hands, not knowing at which point they would be shot down by the Indians by an ambush or lurking behind some wall. We often think we live in evil times, but the blessings we enjoy can't be enumerated, compared to those of our forefathers.

Henry Weidner's grant to this splendid plantation was taken out in 1750 in the name of the King. The date of the Rock House was taken in 1750 in the same way. The other Plantations belonging to Henry Weidner, along with these two beautiful rivers were patented afterwards. He had three sons and five daughters. The names of the sons are Daniel, Henry and Abram, the latter was killed during the Revolutionary War. He had five daughters, whose names were Mary, who married Lightfoot Williams; Barbara, who married John Dellinger; Elizabeth, who married Henry

Summerow. Catherine, who married John Muell; Mollie, who married Jesse Robinson. He gave his rock house to Henry, who later sold it to Jacob Summey and moved to Missouri. To Daniel he gave Daniel Side's place near where the late George Weidner lived. To his daughter Mary, he gave the place now owned by Major Mull, Esq., and was known as the Lightfoot William's place. To Elizabeth, he gave part of the Mull land. To Catherine, he gave the lands occupied by the Mulls on Jacob's Fork. He deeded his homeplace to Jesse Robinson, his son-in-law, instead of his daughter Mollie. It is supposed that he agreed to support his father and mother-in-law during their lifetimes. He was a friend of the poor and needy. He distributed his bounty with a liberal hand. He was greatly loved by his neighbors. He lived to a good and ripe old age and died without an enemy. The crowning act of his life (by the pious example of his noble and Christian wife, when the sacrament of the Lord's Supper was being administered to her for the last time in his presence by the Rev. John Fritchey, who saw that he wanted to unite with her celebrating the dying love of his Saxons, asked him if he, too did not want to give himself to Jesus, and he said he did.) was joining the magnificent domains in the hands of the descendants of the great pioneer, who for honesty, integrity, and correct living, is not surpassed by any kindred deed or any people. The descendants of Henry Weidner should be proud of their record. They have showed themselves equal in every emergency; naturally modest and unobtrusive, but when occasion required, they were bold and daring.

The lessons gleaned from this service, which are important not only as history but also as an insight into the character and traits that saw these immigrant settlers through some of the most trying times, are difficult to grasp. Their sense of courage and devotion to family continue to be passed down to subsequent generations.

Regarding family legacy, it is important to recognize that the marriage of Elizabeth Weidner on October 8, 1827, to Henry Summerour II (1759–1836) set in motion a series of events that would carry the Summerour family to Georgia. From that marriage came 11 children, the oldest being Henry Summerour III (1787–1848), who later would move to Georgia and become active in the Georgia Gold Rush of the 1830s. After Mary Weidner died, Henry began to deed various farm properties he owned to his children, which, in a way, made him his own executor. This included a bequest of a large farm to Elizabeth and Henry II. We suppose that the gains from the sale of this land were eventually used by their sons Henry II and John to begin their new life in Georgia. It is very likely that their religious roots in the Lutheran Church bear evidence of their reliance on faith, which no doubt helped them endure times of hardship and work and which obviously paid off for them and the generations that followed.

No recounting of the events of this period could adequately capture the backdrop of our ancestors' push from their homeland to a foreign frontier to forge a new beginning out of almost nothing. Their spirit and resolve cannot be overstated. Acquiring new land, building homes, and developing methods to sustain themselves must have taken a strength of character which nearly defies understanding. Nevertheless, they persisted, and with faith and hard work they carved out a life for themselves and for generations to follow. No doubt they came to depend on each other—a trait that accompanied the Summerour name and became their source of strength and determination. Family loyalty and a love for kinship would continue to mold and grow their progeny far beyond these pioneer beginnings.

Sommerau village

Henry II marker

Heinricch S. Marker

A List of Foreigners, imported in the Ship Patience, Capt. John Brown. Qualified Sept. 16, 1748.

[List 122 C] At the Courthouse at Philadelphia, 16 September 1748.

Present: Joshua Maddox, Septimus Robinson, } Esquires

The Foreigners whose Names are underwritten, imported in the Ship Patience, John Browne, Master, from Rotterdam, but last from Cowes, did this day take the usual Oaths to the Government

Adam Böhringer
Andreas Böhringer
Johannes Schmidt
Conradt LeÜbbel
Heinrich Sumerauer
Johannes Zobinger
Hans Wanger
Stephan (X) Wenger

Hans Adam Kunckel, Senior
Hans Adam Kunckel, Junior
Hans Kunckel
Johannes Summerauer
Anthoni Weinkoten
Matthäis Burger
Jacob Haller

Passenger List

Sommerau sign

Henry III marker 2021

Chapter 3

Hightower or Frogtown

Generations 4, 5

"Harrison seems to have been a leader all his life."[20]

~Ben F. Summerour

The veracity of the above statement is evidenced by Harrison's keen sense of judgment regarding life's crossroads—decisions that had a profound impact on his entire family. As Auraria's mines began to close in 1848, Harrison made the choice to follow goldmining to a nearby area as well as to open a store in the Hightower/Frogtown community along the Etowah River in northwest Forsyth County, Georgia. In 1849 he moved, along with his wife, Mary Ann, to a large farmhouse in Hightower, where over the next 25 years they would raise their 9 children. There was no guarantee that without hard work and persistence they would be able to overcome the hardships of life in this region. The period of 1835 to 1850 was a very tumultuous time and was greatly affected by events such as the Indian removal and the Georgia land lottery, which changed many aspects of daily life as well as the fortunes and future of both Cherokees and white men.

In the 50 years prior to Harrison and his family's arrival, the community of Hightower had faced many of the same challenges as Auraria. Hardships and trials were brought on by conflict with the Cherokee Indians—and the Cherokees' eventual removal—confusion over land ownership created by the 1932 Land Lottery, and the struggle to find gold. Harrison had taken his family from one distressed area to another, but he did not seem to be daunted by all that he faced.

Hightower, or Hightower Crossroads as it is sometimes called, was along the "Federal Road"—originally known as the "Georgia Road"—which allowed travel from Nashville to Savannah and was intended to benefit the Cherokees under a promise in a previous treaty. Although called the Federal Road, none of its construction was done by the federal government, as those in its path would be the ones to benefit from it.

The "road" was not much wider than a path able to accommodate men on horseback, wagons, or foot. In some ways the road was a symbol of the inevitable conflict between Cherokees and European settlers. Some portions of the road were cleared by Cherokees, giving them[21] a path through Cherokee land into what is now Forsyth County, Georgia, along the Etowah River. This made Hightower both a prominent location for travelers and a viable marketplace for Cherokees and white settlers, particularly, those who came to try mining there.[22] That section of the Federal Road would one day be forever marked as part of the original "Trail of Tears," but not until much history would be played out there. As of this writing, a section of road now called Old Federal Road and Georgia Highway 369 (Matt Highway) still exists and cuts across the Etowah River near where Hightower once stood. While this region has begun to see a certain measure of development today, most of it is still farmland, and the sites of the old stores and taverns are now woodlands. One notable site is a large landfill which serves Forsyth County.

From 1800 to 1850 Hightower was established as a center of commerce and a sometimes government outpost. Jacob Scudder was one of the earliest white men to settle among the Cherokees, putting him in a unique position in that, although he was their friend and supporter, he—along with many educated white and mixed-blood men—eventually concluded that the best course of action for the Cherokees would be to move West. But before this happened, Scudder had established himself as a merchant and trader at Hightower. Trading with the Indians was generally forbidden, but Scudder was able to gain a license to do business with them, and he did so for several years. In the late 1820s Scudder surrendered his original store to George Welch, a mixed-blood Cherokee who was later instrumental in negotiating the Treaty of New Echota (1835), which led to the eventual mass exodus of the Cherokees. Upon surrendering his original store, Scudder simply moved to another location east of the Hightower settlement.[23]

By about 1830 the federal government had become convinced it needed to protect the interests of the Cherokees whose lands had begun to be overrun by white settlers in search of gold, a decision that conflicted with the wishes of the state government. In May of 1830 the U.S. Government contracted with Scudder to build a stockade, known as Camp Eaton, to house those white men who were found to be violating the rights of the Cherokees. They built the barracks and other buildings on 28 acres of Scudder's property with the approval of Secretary of War John Eaton and President Andrew Jackson.

The facility was near Scudder's Inn or "public house," which he had built earlier and which had become well known for its tavern. After about six months, Governor of Georgia George Gilmer was flooded with complaints from citizens, and the federal troops were later withdrawn. As a true sign of the changing attitude toward Cherokees, the state soon agreed to open Camp Gilmer (not to be confused with Fort Gilmer) to be under control of the state militia, with the purpose of sending a military force to the remote outpost "for the protection of the Goldmines and to enforce the laws of the Cherokee Territory."[24] Scudder, being a good businessman, contracted with the state to furnish supplies and merchandise to the encampment. Jacob Scudder proved his wisdom in a letter to Governor Gilmer regarding the plight of the Cherokees:

The progress of human and earthly events has brought it to the question of continued Cherokee occupation to a crisis, when a change must take place in the country. God alone can prevent. We well might lament and mourn for their misfortunes.[25]

Scudder was a state senator and introduced legislation in 1832 that split Cherokee County into several counties. In doing so he thus legislated himself into Forsyth County and so is known as "the first citizen of Forsyth County."[26] He died on March 7, 1870, and was buried in his family cemetery in Frogtown. Unfortunately, the cemetery was later destroyed by vandals who opened his grave, looking for gold—which by then had most likely been lost during the Civil War. The inscription on his tombstone read:

TO THE HONORABLE MEMORY OF
JACOB M. SCUDDER

Who was born in Wilkes County Georgia
the 13th day of July 1798.
Married Diana Jones in Jackson County Georgia
the 7th Day of May 1812.
Moved to the Cherokee Indian Country,
now Forsyth County Georgia in 1815.
Departed this life March 7th, 1870.
Ages 81 Ys, 7 Mo, 6 Days
But his life was as correct as most men.27

One of the most well-known and referenced businesses in Hightower is Blackburn's Tavern. Known in those days as a "public house and stand," its proprietor was Lewis Blackburn, who had settled in the area after the War of

1812. A white man whose family had married into the Cherokees, "he was a well-to-do farmer, miller, merchant, public housekeeper, and slave holder, with extensive land holdings and improvements on both sides of the Hightower (now Etowah) River, where he also opened a public ferry at the Federal Road crossing."[28] Many who regularly traveled the Federal Road often stopped at Blackburn's for a night of rest, food, and drinks. Its most famous guest was President James Monroe, who along with his secretary of war, John C. Calhoun, stopped there in 1819 while touring the area. Since Blackburn was a white man with Cherokees in his family, he, as all others in a similar situation, was stripped of his holdings, including his store, ferry, and mill, in 1835–36. Like others, he was able to later apply for reparations from the federal fund used to support the many Cherokee families who were in many cases similarly treated. Blackburn also applied for Georgia citizenship, which was approved by the Georgia Legislature. Later, he migrated to Oklahoma, probably to join his kin, including his seven quarter-blood daughters and their families. He died in 1841 in Chelsea, Rogers County, Oklahoma. Many of his relatives and family are buried in the Blackburn Cemetery in Hightower near the Etowah River.

Another well-known public house on the Federal Road was one owned by Thomas Buffington. Appearing soon after the road was opened around 1806, Buffington's Tavern is infamously known as the site where James Vann, the most well-known countryman of mixed-blood of that era, was killed. He was an English-speaking half-blood who played an important part in Cherokee history. Because of his heritage, Vann had a unique place both in the world of the white men and in his Cherokee community. However, he was widely known to be very ruthless and cruel to those with whom he associated. He bragged often about having killed several people during his lifetime.

Around midnight on February 20, 1809, after spending several days drinking at Buffington's Tavern, he "stepped out of the tavern and stood before the open door"[29] when someone shot and killed him. Vann had lived a short but volatile life of 43 years and died from an unknown assailant who could have been either Cherokee or a white man, as Vann was equally despised by both. An inscription on a pine board monument says what needs to be known about James Vann:

Here lies the body of James Vann
Who killed many a white man
At last by a rifle ball he fell
And the devil dragged him down to hell.[30]

Vann's gravesite in the Blackburn Cemetery near the Etowah River has often been vandalized and pilfered, but it was also the site of at least two exhumations over the years.[31] So many were enamored and intrigued by this man who lived such a storied life that they could not leave him alone in death. His homeplace, known as the Chief Vann House, is now a Georgia State Park, located on 600 acres near Chatsworth, Murray County, Georgia.

Buffington's Tavern lives on to remember those times, as it was later moved to the Forsyth County Fairgrounds in Cumming in Forsyth County, Georgia.

Questions about the origin of Harrison's own store center around its location as well as the history of the previous owners. The actual site seems to have been a one-half-acre parcel of Land Lot 278, which was designated as such as a result of the 1832 Land Lottery. According to the writings of Don Shadburn, a noted author and expert on the times, the following timeline shows who owned that property as this area transitioned through the land lottery and the Cherokees' removal:

1815: Jacob Scudder, widely known as one of the first white settlers and merchants. After the War of 1812, it is well established that he opened a store on the Federal Road shortly after moving there.

1820s: After operating this store for many years, Scudder had continual conflict with the Cherokee Council over his rights to trade with them, and he sold the store to George Welch (perhaps because he was a Cherokee chief). Scudder then opened his second store, located to the east of the Hightower settlement, which was a site of much Cherokee activity and later was the location of Camp Eaton and Camp Gilmer.

1836: George Welch, because of his Cherokee heritage, was forced to surrender his property, including the store, under the land lottery. It was claimed by Augustus Hodges of Butts County, who in turn sold it to Jesse Hodges and Clinton Porter, also of Butts County, for $200 on August

6, 1836. They in turn told the store to Joshua Holden of Forsyth County for $200 on September 17, 1836.

1837: Joshua Holden sold the property on October 25, 1837, to Madison E. Hudson, son-in-law of Lewis Blackburn.

1838: Madison E. Hudson on February 21, 1838, sold a one-half-acre tract on the southwest corner of Lot 278 to Ambrose Blackburn (Lewis Blackburn's brother or father) for $5.00. Ambrose Blackburn either died or moved without disposing of the "store lot," because in August 15, 1838, Hudson sold the same one-half-acre lot to Washington F. Archer of Anderson District, South Carolina.

1841: Washington Archer, while living in Rutherford County, Tennessee, on April 5, 1841, sold the one-half-acre lot to William C. Field, a pioneer schoolteacher in the area, for $5.00.

1844: As a result of a lawsuit and judgment against William C. Field, Sheriff Absalom Thornton, "at public outcry," sold the lot to Oliver Strickland on July 2, 1844.

1846: Talbot Strickland, brother and administrator of Oliver Strickland's estate, on September 10, 1846, sold the lot and other property to Hardy J. Strickland.

1848: Hardy J. Strickland operated the store for two years, and on April 18, 1848, sold it to George Cowen and John S. Oliver (brother-in-law of Lewis Blackburn).

1849: Cowan and Oliver sold the one-half-acre lot, along with 13 of the 40 acre lots, to Harrison Summerour on January 4, 1849. Harrison operated the store as well as continuing to mine gold in the area.

1874: Harrison Summerour sold the store to James L. Heard, whose daughter Martha Emma Heard (1865–1933) married Charles William Summerour (1865–1953), son of Harrison and Mary Summerour, on December 24, 1891, which was three years prior to the sale of the store.

Note: It is not clear which owners operated a store on the site.

One of the many legacies of Frogtown, as it is often called, is the close nature of the various families who lived there and owned businesses which they often bought and sold to each there. There are several examples of marriages between these families which cemented their relationships forever, as noted between the Heard and Summerour families. They no doubt trusted each other, as there are instances where a member of one family acted as agent for another one in land transactions. Most of all there must have been respect for each of these families, who impacted each other and this unique time in history.

Mining was still active in the area, and the most successful and long-lasting mine of this era was likely the Franklin or Creighton Mine near Ball Ground. The background of its history came from the land lottery in 1832, when a widow, Mary A. Franklin, acquired a 40-acre tract. When she began to get offers for the property, she decided to look for herself, and when she arrived at the location, she found miners who were digging away on what was now her land. She proceeded to evict them and, with her family under her leadership, began mining. No records are available, but it is estimated that they mined a million dollars in gold around 1880. Later, the mine was owned by J. M. Creighton, who operated it until 1911. The site of the mine is now privately owned but still intrigues mineral hunters to this day.

At the time they moved to Hightower in 1849, Harrison was 34, Mary Ann was 21, and their first son, John Henry Summerour (1850–1903), the writer's great-grandfather, was one month old, as evidenced by census data from that year. Interestingly, the data reveals two young men who were in the household, S. R. Henderson, age 23, and T. J. Hightower, age 20, who are both identified as "merchants," indicating they were involved in the Frogtown store from the beginning. S. R. Henderson was Mary Ann's brother, and Thomas J. Hightower, born in Tennessee in 1831, would later, in 1854, marry Elizabeth E. Henderson, sister of Mary Ann. This made him Harrison's brother-in-law as well as business partner.

One factual question that had to be answered for me was whether there was any connection between the place name Hightower and Thomas Hightower. From information provided by the Bell Research Center at the Forsyth County History Center, the name apparently goes back as far as 1819 and could possibly have been from another resident who lived there around that time. It is worth noting that Thomas Hightower's family later founded Hightower Box and Tank Company in Atlanta.

One tangible piece of history, which I now possess, is a daybook or ledger from the Hightower store. Because of its rarity and importance in our family history, the "ledger or store book," as it was referred to in my family, has been passed down to me and is now kept in a safe place to preserve and protect it. The book lists daily transactions for each day from May to September in 1851. The transactions provide names of those who lived and shopped there. About 2014 it was loaned to the Forsyth County Historical Society at the Bell Research Center in Cumming, Georgia. While it was in their possession, they copied and transcribed it to allow others to have access to the data, which in many ways was a list of those who lived and traded in that area during that period. The time spent looking through the ledger and comparing pricing and seeing the interesting items is a pastime many members of our family have enjoyed through the years, and it is one which the writer hopes will continue to be a treasured part of recorded history.

Ledger entries for May 31, 1851. Hightower

Hardy Hendrix 1 Glass Whiskey		*1.00*	
1 pair boots		*3.50*	
3- brown drills		*.45*	*4.05*
Thomas Whisenant 1 Pad lock		*.20*	
1-Funnel		*.10*	
A .J. Kemp 2 weeding hoes		*.85*	
William Holdbrooks 2 pad locks		*.50*	
Caleb Ellis 1 lb. ginger		*.10*	
H. Summerour goods		*1.65*	
Henry Strickland 4 yds of shirting		*4.00*	
2 glass jars		*1.00*	
1 small glass jar		*.57*	*5.37*
William Holdbrooks 1 wool hat		*1.37*	
½ lb. powder		*.20*	
1 weeding hoe		*.75*	*2.32*

Harrison and Mary Ann had 9 children, all of whom were born and raised in Hightower. Two infant boys died very young, one at 16 months and the other at 9 months, as shown below. Later, the lives of some of Harrison and Mary Ann's surviving children will be detailed in honor and respect for their impact on so many of my generation. The following is a listing of their genealogical data:

John Henry*—the author's great-grandfather—was born in 1850 in Forsyth County, Georgia, and died in 1903 in Milton County, Georgia, now Fulton County. He married Catherine Hope on January 1, 1870. They had six children: Harrison (1871-1954); John Henderson (1877-1950); Frank (1884-1957); Patrick W. (1890-1958); Guy (1893-1971); and Charles Anderson (1875-1953), who is the author's grandfather and namesake;

Franklin Reese Henderson was born May 5, 1853, and died August 1, 1854 (age 1 year and 4 months).

Milton Harrison was born May 17, 1855, and died January 8, 1856 (age 9 months).

Henry Harrison was born May 21, 1871, and died November 11, 1954. Married Junia Elizabeth Rogers (daughter of Augustus Rogers), born May 15, 1876, and died June 10, 1970. Both are buried in Lucedale, Mississippi. Junia Rogers was a mixed blood of Cherokee descent, which is the only known such marriage in the Summeour lineage. Shortly after marrying, they moved to Lucedale, Mississippi, where they had 10 children: Florence Etna (1894–1993); Margaret Katherine (1897–1973); Milton Harrison (1899–1891); Samuel Nelson (1901–1921); Mary Ethel (1903–1992); Augustus Rogers (1907–1982); John Henry (1909–1943); Sara Elizabeth (1912–2008); Martha Emily (1914–1992); and Kenneth Hope (1920–1997).

Charles William (Will) was born January 20, 1857, and died 1930. Married Emma Heard in 1883. She was born in 1895 and died in 1953. They had 8 children: Susan Parale (1885–1982); James Heard (1888–1958); Steven Harrison (1890–1980); Mary Ruth (1893–1996); Nellie Ruth (1896–1988); Charles William Jr. (1899–1987); Annie Kate (1901–1972); Charlotte (1904–1988). Will and Emma are buried in the Duluth Church Cemetery in Duluth, Gwinnett County, Georgia.

Thomas Edward (Tom Ed) was born in 1869 and died in 1925. Married first to Annie Clark and then to Margaret Eulalia (Lala) Simpson, who was born in 1871 and died in 1960. They had one daughter, Annie Summerour. Tom Ed and Lala are buried in the Norcross City Cemetery, Norcross, Gwinnett County, Georgia. Summerour Middle School was named for Lala Simpson Summerour, who donated the property for the school and Norcross High School, which was later demolished and rebuilt in another area.

Jefferson Davis (Jeff) was born November 10, 1869 and died in 1932; He married Nancy Kelly (1861–1939) in

Wilbarger County, Texas. They moved to Vernon, Texas, before 1910 and lived their entire lives there. Both are buried in the Eastview Memorial Park in Vernon, Texas.

Mary Ann* was born November 18, 1863, and died in 1887 at age 23. She was known to be very active in teaching at the Warsaw Methodist Church. She never married.

Homer Hightower* was born October 7, 1866, and died September 30, 1915. Married in 1887 to Susan Elizabeth Mitcham, who was born in 1869 and died in 1920.* They had 4 children: an infant son (1886–1886); Jeff (1888–1927); Mary K., (1889-1916); Benjamin F., (1891–1982), and Joseph. Edwin (1905–1972). Ben Summerour compiled a history of the Summerour Family in 1965 which became my inspiration and source of much of our family history, much of which is incorporated into this writing. His compilation and recording were done prior to the internet age and are a wonderful example of why history should be recorded.

Susan Elizabeth* was born in 1859 and died in 1954. She married John Newton McClure Sr* (1862–1927). They had 7 children: Robert Ed (1888–1927); Emma (1890–1894); Hallie (1892–1960); John Newton Jr. (1899–1984); Mary (1901–1974); Katherine (1905–1918); Susan Lois (1908–1930). Susie took care of her mother, Mary Ann, until her death in 1913. As had been planned earlier, they lived with her in the family homeplace (known as the old Brick House).

**Denotes buried in the family plot in the Warsaw Church Cemetery along with Harrison and Mary Ann, in now what is Johns Creek (also known as Warsaw) in Fulton County, Georgia.*

Harrison would spend almost 25 years in Hightower, raising his family and continuing to be a merchant there as well as mining gold. He was appointed postmaster in 1848 and served until 1866, when mail service was discontinued. In 1871 his son John Henry became postmaster. Harrison was also active in mining operations, dividing his time between quartz and placer mining or washing down the banks of the river into sluice boxes or dredging sand from the river, using his own boat. His success is evidence that "of the numerous mines scattered throughout the county, (Forsyth) the following presented the highest profits according to the U.S. Mint in Dahlonega: Harrison Summerour, Hardy Strickland, George Kelly, Leroy Howard, Tolbert S. Strickland, Choppy Wellborn, Henry Strickland, and Noah Storey."[32]

During his time in Hightower, Harrison was obviously aware of the fact that they were in an area and time in which local governments did not have the necessary resources to construct public buildings. Family history notes that he, John L., and Franklin loaned money to Dawson County to construct their courthouse in 1860 and then supervised its construction. However, Dawson County history says that "Harrison Summerour, John McAfee, and R. N. McClure secured a bond of $9,000 to construct the courthouse. As the money came into the county, however, the contractors were to be paid, and a difficulty arose and $2,500 was borrowed from Mr. Summerour to meet the deadline of a contract payment."[33]

Under either version, Harrison played a key role in this building, which is now on the National Registry of Historic Places and home to the Dawson County Historical Society. Some family history says that both John L. and Harrison were involved in the building of the Lumpkin County Courthouse in Dahlonega, which is quite possible, as they were very active in gold mining during the time it was built in 1836 and later renovated. It too is on the National Registry of Historical Places as well as being home to the Dahlonega Gold Mine Museum.

As this time in Hightower included the time of the Civil War, while it is somewhat difficult to determine the impact it had on the residents there, it is certain many of them served either in the Army of the Confederacy or the Georgia Militia. In any case, their lives and fortunes would never be the same, as many lives were lost and families displaced over the course of the war. While we do not know the exact impact the war had on Harrison's wellbeing, we note that in his obituary of 1888, "he was worth $250.00 before the Civil War."[34] We can only wonder what his fortune was like in later years, although it does appear that he continued to be known as a wealthy man who had a lot of gold.

One of the legacies of Hightower that had always intrigued and confused me was that the name Frogtown seemed to be synonymous with it, both from my family's stories and from written histories. Ironically, it seems that the record of the origin of the name Frogtown came to be recorded in the diary of John Lafayette Summerour, Harrison's brother. He recounts that "one Sunday James Kell came into Hightower and began drinking, going from one establishment to another, where whiskey flowed freely, and a tall glassful could be bought for ten cents. At last, very intoxicated, Kell staggered out of one of the establishments and yelled loudly to several pass-erby [sic], --"They ought to call this place Frogtown."[35] So now we know, and the name stuck, to be recorded and remembered forever.

Here again, we can clearly see the many attributes of Harrison that marked his life in Frogtown. His vison and business acumen are evident, as shown in his entre-preneurship and his ability to manage many business interests at the same time. And from all appearances, he was generally successful in most of them. He was making money gold mining at a time when mining had taken a downturn. That no doubt required constant management and oversight, which seems to be his strength. Along with his business interests, he and Mary Ann raised a family of 9, who from all accounts were upstanding, as shown by the fact that their oldest, John Henry, became postmaster in Hightower in 1871, following in his father's footsteps, as Harrison had previously been the postmas-ter. Being a successful business- and family man certainly prepared the Summerour family for its next move, which was a two-year period when they lived in Cumming, Forsyth County, Georgia. After living there for that short period, they relocated to Warsaw (now Johns Creek), Milton County (now Fulton) in 1875.

Photo circa 1890s. *(from an article by Martha Hogan Avett in North Georgia History)*
Scudder's Inn in Hightower (Frogtown), Georgia. After Scudder. Harrison Summerour and his family here before moving in around 1875 to the Warsaw community (now Johns Creek GA).

Summerour Hightower house

Dawson County Courthouse

Frogtown Store

Lumpkin County Courthouse 2021

CHAPTER 4

The Old Brick House

Warsaw - Johns Creek - Forsyth County - Milton County - Fulton County

Generations 4, 5

After raising a large family and having continued success as a merchant, farmer, and goldminer around Hightower, in about 1873 Harrison moved his family a short distance away to Cumming, the seat of Forsyth County. Following a two-year stay there, he began to look for other opportunities in order to provide for his family. In 1875 he bought a 581-acre farm with a large brick house, barns, and more in Warsaw, then known as Milton County, Georgia (known now as Johns Creek in Fulton County, Georgia). At the time, Harrison was age 61 and his wife, Mary Ann, was 47. Their oldest son, John H., 25, had married Catherine Hope, 24, while they lived in Hightower. When they married they moved in with the rest of the family, as was common at that time. Except for the brief stay in Cumming, all the children had been born and raised in Hightower and were probably confident in their father, who had made a similar decision 25 years earlier to leave Auraria after its demise. Although they had no known connection to their new town, the decision to move was undoubtedly made easier due to the family's wealth. Still, it was most assuredly a real task to move all household and family possessions over 20 miles with only horse and wagon.

The above place names have all at various times been used to describe the location where Harrison Summerour moved his large family in 1875. This area was originally part of the large Cherokee Nation that had been divided into 10 counties in 1832, one of which—Forsyth County—included a small community known as Warsaw. In 1858 this area was incorporated into Milton County, and in 1932 Milton County was merged into Fulton County, which included the city of Atlanta and sections of the county both north and south of the city proper. In 2006, after a vote by its residents and approval by the Georgia Legislature, the city of Johns Creek was formed and immediately became one of the top-10 largest and most wealthy cities in the state.

However, in 1875 this now-wealthy area was only sparsely populated by family farms, which included many people who had been deeply affected by the Civil War just a few years prior. One of these was Jackson Graham, a relative of the wealthy Howell family, who had unfortunately lost his farm and large brick home to bankruptcy. As mentioned, in 1875 Harrison Summerour purchased this brick home and 581 acres for $5,000 from the bankruptcy court. He moved many of his children—and later, three grandchildren from John and Catherine—into what the family would long refer to as "the old brick house." Jackson Graham and Harrison became and remained good friends.

"The old brick house" has long been the intrigue of many. It was a stately brick home, without question one of a kind in its time. It was initially known as the Howell Mansion, as it had been built by Judge Clark Howell (1811-1882) and later occupied by others in his family.

Judge Howell built the house in about 1849 and lived there for a few years before he moved to Marthasville shortly before Marthasville became Atlanta. Judge Clark Howell was known as such because he was the first judge to hold office in this era. His father, Evan Howell, had come to the area in 1820, and Judge Howell's son Captain Evan Park Howell (1839-1905) served in the Civil War, including the battle of Atlanta. After the war Captain Howell purchased the *Atlanta Constitution* newspaper, which he and his son Clark Howell (1863-1936) owned and edited for the next 50 years, growing it to great prominence, including winning a Pulitzer Prize.

The "Howell Mansion" was constructed—most likely by slaves—of bricks taken from a site adjacent to the house. Its style and construction were distinctive, and its location was quite prominent, despite the nearly inconceivable changes which would eventually occur there in future years. The property's proximity to the Chattahoochee River, only a mile away, made it a prime place for farming, which was the predominant use of all such properties in the area. The river would become the site of numerous ferries used to transport people and goods into nearby Gwinnett County and beyond.

Many at the time concluded that the house was haunted, or as Ben Summerour (Harrison's grandson) said, it had "haints" [sic]. Ben recalled playing there as a young boy with his cousins, who like him were somewhat taken aback when Grandmother Mary Ann forbade them from going into an upper room. As Ben's account of the story goes:

> *We grandchildren were quite small, and there was no better place to go than Grandma Summerour's, and of course the McClure children were our first cousins. You see, this applied to all the grandchildren; often two or three sets would be there at the same time. During the trials of the years after the Civil War, Grandma of necessity as well as doubtless by nature a very frugal type, saved everything possible yet lived liberally with a good orchard of peaches and apples, with walnuts and other things to store – all in the upstairs room. Grandma always kept the key to the lock on the door to the room upstairs where the "haints" stayed, along with all those good things – apples, peanuts, popcorn and many sacks of black walnuts. Well, the haints did not bluff the boys too much, just so we could find a ladder high enough to the reach the second-story window in the room where the haints lived, and provided Grandma was not too close around. The room was full of many things which the other boys kept trying to find. So much*

for the story, which some little pre-kindergarten child even today believes, as it was to all of us just prior to or around the turn of the 1900s.

Importantly, the house would be home for all the Summerour children until they left the roost, which was often years after they married and started their own families. This arrangement, very common in those times, was of necessity as it allowed the boys to aide in the farming—the primary source of livelihood. Harrison was also known to have been a large slaveholder throughout his life, but at the time he moved to Warsaw, thankfully, all slaves had been released. Since he was wealthier than most, Harrison was later able to help at least three of his sons find farms in the area, making them the largest landowners in area. This is detailed in the following chapter.

After Harrison's death in 1888, his youngest daughter, Susan Elizabeth (1869–1954)—or "Aunt Susie" as she was often referred to by my father—lived with her mother until Mary Ann died in 1911. Susan had married John N. McClure in 1867, a man who by all accounts was revered by all and, most importantly, by his mother-in-law. Because the house did not have modern conveniences, in 1910 or early 1911, they all moved to a more modern house in Norcross. It was there that Mary Ann died on May 8, 1911. The McClure family lived in Norcross for many years following, and John was quite successful in the fertilizer business as well as farming.

But their legacy was most certainly left in Warsaw. The name of the road and bridge which crossed the

Chattahoochee River—and passed by "the old brick house"—became known as McClure Bridge Road, and even today, a small stretch of it remains in Duluth, although the streets there have been reconfigured and, in some cases, taken on other names.

Upon leaving the brick house, according to Ben Summerour, the family turned it and the operation of the McClure farm over to the farm's foreman. Susie McClure would go on to live longer than any in her family, dying on May 22, 1954, at the age of 85. She is buried in the family cemetery at Warsaw alongside several generations of the McClure family.

While the legacy of a person is often flattering and sometimes overstated, Harrison Summerour's 1888 obituary is genuinely demonstrative of his life of 74 years. The few words below from the *Atlanta Constitution* seem to portray him as simply as the life he lived.

Harrison Summerour Obituary

On Friday, 13th, at his home in Warsaw, Milton County, Mr. Harrison Summerour died after a third stroke of paralysis, and was buried in the old church cemetery near his home. He had reached the age of 74 years and one day. He rose from the cobbler's bench to be worth, before the [Civil] war, more than two hundred fifty thousand dollars. Integrity and honest dealings with his fellow man actuated all his transactions

> throughout his life, always kind to the poor, and lent his hand in substantial aid to meritorious young men.
>
> He never deserted a friend in need.[36]

The purchasing power of $250,000 in 1860 would be over $7.7 million today (2020).[37] While this amount was significantly impacted by the Civil War, it puts Harrison's generosity to his family and those around him into a proper perspective.

On the afternoon of July 18, 1963, as a 14-year-old teenager, my father took me over to Warsaw, and with tears in his eyes, we watched the old brick house where he had once lived crumble from a fire. At the time, no one was living in the house, as it was being used to store hay for one of the local farm families. A story in the *News Herald* – a Lawrenceville, Georgia, newspaper—was headlined, "Once Grand Dwelling Now in Ruins." It was a sad day for all our family, particularly for my father and his brothers, who had spent much of their life there.

But the intrigue of this unique house did not end with its demise. Over the years many who had no connection to its grandeur have inquired and searched its history. One legend goes that Harrison, not one to trust banks, had supposedly buried a cache of gold somewhere on the property. One of my cousins, Joe Summerour, searched the property with a metal detector to no avail, but the story continues to this day. A large church, Perimeter Presbyterian (or Perimeter Church), today sits on a good portion of the original farm. When my daughter and her family joined this church in 2010, they were told by church leaders that they suspected there might still be gold buried on the property. At that time she was not aware this was once family property—although now you know another motivation for my writing this book.

My memories of the Warsaw (Johns Creek) area go back to my teenage years after the farm property passed down to my father's generation. To contrast the landscape then to today would be impossible for me and unimaginable for my father and his brothers. The entire section of the original 581 acres has been developed by almost all commercial and residential means possible, including a large shopping center with a Starbucks, restaurants, and a movie theater at 9700 Medlock Bridge Road, Johns Creek. The only topography still identifiable is a large oak tree, easily visible in photos of the house. And even though I only saw the house in its later years, "the old brick house" will always hold a special place in my memory. And it will no doubt continue to hold intrigue for many generations to come.

The Summerour family's impact, particularly regarding their farms and real estate, is easily seen today by examining the various outcomes and uses of the land as detailed in the following chapter. But for the family unit itself, it was a time to expand their territory and to provide for their numerous offspring, spurring the growth of numerous successful businesses via the four family farms and beyond. However, the common ethic, as exhibited in prior generations, was a desire that all family members could find success and provide for themselves and future generations. All of us who have come after them should appreciate their care and stewardship for each other.

Not wanting to leave a summary of Harrison Summerour's life up to me, consider instead the words of his grandson, Ben:

> *Harrison's life was filled with his aiding his kinfolk, as well as many others, even financial difficulties, with never a hard bargain of which anyone ever heard, as far as I know. He died in 1888 – a man well-liked by all – somewhat austere but warm.*

On Friday, 13th, at his home at Warsaw, Milton county, Mr. Harrison Sainmeraur died from a third stroke of paralysis, and was buried at the old church cemetery near his home. He had reached the age of 74 years and one day. He rose from the cobbler's bench to be worth, before the war, over two hundred thousand dollars. Integrity and honorable dealings with his fellowman actuated all his transactions through life, always kind to the poor and lent his hand in substantial aid to meritorious young men. He never deserted a friend in need.

Atlanta Constitution
January 18, 1888
www.newspapers.com

Harrison's Obituary

Brick House painting by Sandra Boles Lamar

THE NEWS-HERALD LAWRENCEVILLE, GA. THURSDAY, JULY 18, 1963

Once Grand Dwelling Now In Noble Ruins

Brick House Burns, 1963

CHAPTER 5

The Summerour Farms

Warsaw – John's Creek – Johns Creek

Generations 5, 6

The various Summerour farms of the late 1880s truly were working farms, which is important to understand as we view their impact on the modern-day city of Johns Creek, Georgia. The fact that the Summerour families resided on and made their living from this land should help present-day citizens understand and respect the places where they now shop, eat, worship, and live. As we view what the real estate has become, hopefully, the reader will also learn to appreciate the character of the individuals who farmed the land, were loyal and helpful to their neighbors, and served their community well. To do so would not only be appropriate, it would also fulfill my accepted obligation to honor and show respect for my ancestors and their impact on the world then and today.

Each farm had its own story, and this chapter is a glimpse into each one, uncovering what is known about the land and those who made it their home and sustenance.

Harrison Summerour Farm

On June 15, 1875, Harrison Summerour purchased 581 acres made up of fourteen, 40-acre lots plus a 21-acre river lot. He acquired these after Jackson Graham (1815-1887) lost the property in bankruptcy court after struggles following the Civil War. Graham was married to Julian Rebecca Howell (1822-1911), sister of Clark F. Howell, builder of "the old brick house" located there (also known as the Howell Mansion). She was the daughter of Evan Howell (1782-1868), who had moved to the area in 1820 and had started Howell's Crossroads, later—and presently—known as Duluth, Gwinnett County, Georgia.

Despite the financial entanglements involved, Harrison and Jackson Graham later became good friends, and in the following year, 1876, Harrison loaned Graham's wife, Julian (Julia) Rebecca Graham, $1,667. This allowed her to retain a portion of the property lost in the bankruptcy. Her brother, Clark F. Howell (also known as Judge Howell), had been able to purchase a part of the tract as well. However, within a year Julian sold some of the property to Robert N. Medlock to pay off some other debts. Land records reflect that Harrison often loaned money to neighbors, making him a friend and confidant of many. He seemed to do so with the most integrity possible, although he was still able to balance the financial and personal aspects of each such instance, always considering the property as collateral.

Over the next few years, Harrison sold off small parcels to various individuals, including one and a half acres to

H. B. Moulder in 1877 for a building lot and three acres to Edward S. Lamb in 1878. In 1881 he gave one acre to the leaders of Concord Baptist Church for use as a school or church, with the provision that "if the church should be vacated at any time and not used for the purposes stated, the title shall be null and void."

As of this writing in 2020, Concord Baptist Church continues to exist at 9400 Medlock Bridge Road (Georgia Highway 141). In 1882 Harrison purchased 341 acres that was part of the property of Henry C. Rogers, who lost it in a bankruptcy. The purchase included Rogers Ferry on the Chattahoochee River.

From the above property and other adjacent or nearby land, Harrison helped his three sons, John Henry in 1880, Charles William in 1880, and Homer Hightower in 1887, establish large farms which became their homeplaces and working farms. Each of these will later be described in detail. As shown in earlier years, Harrison was very loyal and caring to many around him, especially to his family. There is no question that the original farm was a working farm, as the 1880 Population Census listed John H., Charles W., and Thomas E. as "farmers" on his farm. The scope of his farming activity is shown in the 1889 Agricultural Census, which lists 79 farm laborers hired by Harrison, indicating Harrison's success, unlike many smaller framers who had lost their property or had converted them to tenant farms staffed by sharecroppers. The same agricultural census lists a large number of horses and mules, 9 cows, 120 chickens, and production of 20 tons of hay, with 60 acres in Indian corn, 8 acres of rye, 15 acres of wheat, and orchards of apple trees which produced 300 bushels of apples, peaches, and other fruit. In addition, it would be expected that they also raised many acres of cotton, although the census does not include cotton crops.

After Harrison's death in 1888, his will provided that ownership be vested in his wife, Mary Ann, who, along with her daughter Susan (Susie) and son-in-law John N. McClure, would continue to live in the brick house. The McClure family later moved to Norcross to better provide for Susie's mother in the days before her death in 1911. According to the writings of Ben Summerour, grandson of Harrison and Mary Ann, the McClures provided the brick house to their farm supervisor and continued to operate the farm, including a cotton gin and sawmill.[38] Also in the 1930s my grandfather, Charles A. would move his family into the house while he operated the farm he inherited from his father, John Henry.

For the present-day reader's perspective, Harrison's farm generally consisted of the property at the corner of what is now Medlock Bridge Road and State Bridge Road, the current site of numerous restaurants, retail stores, and a movie theater. The property ran along Medlock Bridge and continued past what is now Old Alabama Road, including the Atlanta Athletic Club and their property across the street, currently used mainly as a parking lot. Needless to say, no one from earlier generations could have ever imagined this area as it now exists.

John Henry Summerour Farm

John Henry (1850–1903) marred Catherine Hope (1861–1905) and their children were Henry Harrison (1871–1954), Charles Anderson (1875–1953), Franklin Reese (1884–1957), John Henderson (1887–1950), Patrick Walter (1890–1968), and Guy (1893–1971). It is noteworthy that John Henderson is referred to as "John, Jr." in his father's will, obvious evidence that wills were usually scribed by non-family members who used prescribed text used in many wills of that time.

On April 5, 1880, John Henry, the author's great grandfather, purchased a 510-acre farm along Old Alabama Road from the estate of Singleton Howell, which included a 25% interest in the Waits Ferry on the Chattahoochee River. The Old Alabama Road was used by planters from the adjoining state, who used the road to get their crops to the railroad that had been built through Duluth in 1871. By the time the family moved to this farm, there was to be no question that the boys would be raised on the farm and involved in its operation, as was customary and part of their family's past.

John Henry lived life much like his father and gained a reputation as a good neighbor and friend to many in the community. He was elected to the Milton County School Board, where he served until his death. He died of stomach cancer at the young age of 53. His obituary, obviously written by one of his Masonic friends, tells us much of what we know about his life.

John Henry Summerour Obituary

Mr. John Henry Summerour died last Friday afternoon at 2 o'clock. He had been ill for about a year and for several months and had not left his home in about two months.

On Saturday afternoon his body was laid to rest in the Summerour enclosure in the Warsaw cemetery. After the Methodist burial ceremony was gone through, the Masons interred the body, that beautiful solemn ceremony making a deep impression on the several hundred people present.

Mr. Summerour was fifty-three years old at the time of his death. He leaves a widow and six children, all boys, four of whom are grown, and two who are married. He belongs to one of the best families in North Georgia, the name Summerour being a synonym of prosperity and good friendship. He leaves an estate worth perhaps twenty thousand dollars or more.

In the death of Mr. Summerour, the county has lost one of its finest men and many men have lost a true and loyal friend. His goodness of heart was proverbial and he helped many a struggling man from adversity to prosperity. Himself a hardworking man, his crowning virtue was his love and respect for

> laboring people. He took a deep interest in educational affairs, being a member of the county board of education at the time of his death. Our departed friend was a Mason and Mason indeed. He loved the ancient and sacred mysteries of order, and its great central light was to guide his footsteps and his rule for faith and practice. He ever squared his action by the square of virtue and kept himself within the confines of the sacred circle within which all Masons try to live. He was an affectionate son, a loyal husband, and a tender father and kind brother and he had an unshaken faith in God, and believed in the immortality of the soul, we believe he found sweet rest.
>
> To the bereaved family, we join hundreds of other friends in our profound and heartfelt sympathy.[39]

Although it is not unusual to see flattering tributes like this one, this eulogy helps bring us closer to him and the life he lived. While it would certainly be enlightening to possess more stories about John Henry's life, he lived in a time when personal information was not widely shared, which again shows the importance of families putting their history in writing for future generations to have and appreciate. As a great-grandson, I regret not asking my father and his family more about their grandfather. I do remember my father referring to his uncle John Henderson as "Big Uncle John" in deference to his own brother, John Henry, whom I knew as Uncle John as well. Later, when I saw a photograph of "Big Uncle John," I knew this moniker referred to age and not to height, since he, like most Summerour men, was never even near six feet tall.

The origin of the name of the city of Johns Creek, Georgia, presents what may by some accounts tie it to the Summerour family. The narrative promoted by the city states a possible connection to several other personalities of the day, none of which seem likely, considering history. The city name "Johns Creek" was likely spurred by the name attached to a large office park created in the 1960s which was given the name "Technology Park - Johns Creek." This was the first time the name was used as a place name.40 As a point of discussion, and for future debate, let me take us back to the actual John's Creek – the one with an apostrophe – which is distinct from the name of the modern-day city. Interestingly, as shown in various plats of the area in 1880, the creek crosses the farms of both John Henry Summerour and that of his brother Charles William Summerour. This presents as likely the possibility that the creek acquired its name by a manner which would have been typical in that day: from the name of the property owner. However, according to the records of the Johns Creek Historical Society, the name shows up in some land records as far back as 1830. While this likely means the name has no connection to the Summerour family, I do like to make it known that my family once owned John's Creek (the stream) – literally.

Even if we do not get credit for naming rights, the fact is that in my youth we sometimes spent Sunday afternoons playing in the creek on Old Alabama Road!

It has recently come to my attention that Harrison was a substantial slaveowner, holding as many as 30 slaves at one time, if the 1850 Census is correct. Although these would not have been a part of his farm at Warsaw in the 1870s–80s, they would have worked his land in Forsyth County. (John Henry's history does not show that he ever owned slaves, which is likely accurate since he did not own any property until about 1880.) Although we now know that Harrison held slaves, we do not and cannot know whether he was cruel to them—as many slaveowners were—or treated them as family, as many slaveowners did. We only know how he treated his family and friends and what is written about him. Going by that evidence, I do believe he was a goodly man regarding the servants of his house.

Charles William Summerour Farm

Charles William (1857–1930) and Emma Heard (1865–1953) married in 1853 and had 8 children: Susan Paralee (1895–1982), James Heard (1888–1958), Steven Harrison (1890–1980), Mary Ruth (1893–1966), Nelle (1896–1988), Charles William Jr. (1897–1987), Annie Kate (1901–1972), and Charlotte (1904–1988).

Charles William (Will) and Emma were extremely active in the farming community in the late 1800s and early 1900s in Warsaw, Duluth, and beyond. Their first farm was established when they acquired a 413-acre tract from C. F. and A. M. Howell on Old Alabama Road, just west of and bordering the farm of Will's brother John Henry. Their farm, like many others of that era, depended on tenant sharecroppers, who both lived and worked the farm. We get an interesting glimpse of tenant farming from *The Cotton Renter's Son,* a firsthand account written by George Lester Vaughn, who was a small boy at the time and lived on the Summerour place, along with about 15 other tenant families. He describes their living quarters as a 20′ by 20′ log house which had likely been used by slave laborers during the pre-Civil War period. His description of the farmland was that the upland or hilly portions were quite rocky, while the bottom land along the Chattahoochee River was loamy with much better soil for planting crops. "Mister Willie," as they referred to their landlord, could be quite demanding at times, yet he was always willing to advance them money until they could repay him after the crops were harvested. Vaughn did say that Mister Willie was very particular about his 20 mules and demanded they be put away in the barn each day when they finished working in the fields.[41]

In 1914 Will sold his farm to S. T. Spruill. In 1994 the original C. W. Summerour farmhouse was relocated and restored as part of the current Autrey Mill Nature Preserve and History Center, which often hosts the Johns Creek Historical Society gatherings. Fulton County purchased the house's original site to build the Spruill - Oaks Library, which opened in 1999.

At some point Will moved to Texas for a short time, where he farmed with his brothers, Homer and Jeff. While Will and Homer returned to Georgia, Jeff remained in the Vernon, Texas, area and established one of the Texas branches of the Summerour family.

In 1903 Will and Emma purchased a large farm in Duluth in Gwinnett County, just east of the Chattahoochee River, where they would continue farming for many years. According to family lore, sometime in the 1920s, after a dispute between Will and Emma, Will moved to Rome in Floyd County, Georgia, where he started yet another farm. In the meantime, the family, including son Steven "Harrison" (1890–1980), continued to work the large farm in Duluth. When Will became quite ill, Emma apparently sent for Harrison, and he returned to Duluth, where he died in 1930. Emma died in 1953, and both are buried in the Duluth Church Cemetery.

After Will's father and mother died, their son Harrison, who was well known to me, managed the farm until the early 1960s when he sold the property to a successful real estate developer named Scott Hudgens. Hudgens helped develop this area, which encompassed the high-end thoroughfares now known as Peachtree Industrial Boulevard and Pleasant Hill Road. (Pleasant Hill Road becomes State Bridge Road after crossing into Fulton County.) For his homeplace. Mr. Hudgens carved out about 100 acres, including the original farmhouse. This property still stands on the northeast corner of Peachtree

Industrial Boulevard and Pleasant Hill Road in Duluth and is now owned by Jacquelyn Hudgens, Scott's widow. Mr. Hudgens is also known for donating several hundred acres near Canton in Cherokee County, Georgia, for a national cemetery.

Homer Hightower Summerour Farm

Homer Hightower (1866-1915) married Susie E. Mitcham (1869-1920) and they had four children: Jeff. H. (1888-1927), Mary (1916-1945), Benjamin Franklin (1891-1982), and Joseph Edwin (1905-1972).

Homer established the first portion of his farm in 1887—one year prior to his father's death— when Harrison deeded him 341 acres, which was the lower part of his original farm. In 1889 Homer added 313 acres to his farm by acquiring the adjacent property from Robert N. and M. P. Medlock. For the current-day resident, this property is bisected by Medlock Bridge Road/Georgia Highway 141 and includes the Atlanta Athletic Club property on the west side of the Chattahoochee River.

In many ways Homer and his family would become the most active and advanced farmers in the area. He was the youngest of Harrison's boys and had always been a high achiever. His farming acumen could be considered inherited, but his love of learning would change methods of farming, particularly as related to cotton, both on his farm and across the country. But before he would settle down in Warsaw, he had to satisfy a young man's desire to first see the country. In his early 20s he embarked on a train trip out west, his destination determined only by the amount of ticket money he possessed. When the ticket-taker looked at the map, Vernon, Texas, became his stopping place. Due to his limited resources, he took several menial jobs but wanted to begin farming in the vast Texas plains. So he wrote home for money.

Well, this obviously raised questions with his family, because his father sent Homer's brother Jeff to survey the situation. When Jeff too became enamored with the farming possibilities there, his father decided to send his more conservative son, Tom Ed. In the end—or rather, as a new beginning—the brothers purchased several tracts at 50¢ per acre in the area of Harold, Texas, just outside of Vernon. Homer's stay would only last about two years, but Jeff would establish roots there which still exist.42 This would become one of the Summerour branches who now call Texas home.

Homer was in many ways a very progressive farmer, although at times his family would question some of his ventures that did not meet immediate success. But that never seemed to prevent him from experimenting—a trait which would later bring him fame throughout the farming world. Along the way he raised all types of animal stock, including sheep, hogs, cattle, and horses. At one point he raised sorghum cane to produce syrup, a very desirable product, and even devoted 100 acres to growing it. As for farming practices, he was simply ahead of his time—rotating crops and maximizing yield from the land—giving him a reputation as an innovator.

Homer's experimenting and patience would eventually pay off once he began developing cotton. Real insight comes from the article "History of Half and Half Cotton," published in the *Forsyth County News,* April 7 and April 14, 1949, written by Homer's son, Joseph Edwin Summerour:

> In the first few years after the turn of the century, in 1904-5, Homer bought a small amount of pure Cook cotton seed. He ordered them directly from the breeder. The following fall when the cotton from those seed had matured there was one stalk which attracted his attention. The bolls seemed to be larger, and when they matured and opened, they produced a larger amount of seed cotton. To the touch the cotton itself had a somewhat less silky feeling from the ordinary variety. It felt more like a type of cotton fiber. At once Homer's research went into investigative action. Why was it different?
>
> For a starter he weighed all the locks from one boll on his gold balance scales which he had kept from his gold dredging project. Using Troy weights, he discovered that its weight was a few grams heavier than the usual run of cotton. He then picked the entire stalk taking all the seed from the end and weighing them separately, a boll at a time. The lint from his stalk was heavier than from

> any his brothers and sisters planted in the same field. Next, he picked all the cotton from the entire stalk and separated them by hand. The seed he saved for the next planting in the spring.[43]

From here Homer, with the help of his daughter Mary, continued the process of elimination in order to find the best seed, a time-consuming process which involved weighing them on old gold scales and determining which he should use. To enhance the process, he began to cross-pollinate the seed, and over the next few years perfected what was to become known as Summerour Half and Half Cotton. His cotton produced as much as 50% higher yield, and with his proselytizing, it captured the attention of farmers near and far. With help from his family and others, Homer undertook a national advertising campaign, spreading the news across the country. Homer had nurtured and perfected a novel and industry-changing product.

Unfortunately, Homer did not see it come to complete fruition, as he died on September 30, 1915. However, with sons Jeff, Ben, and Joe surviving him, Half and Half Cotton would thrive for many years to come. Initially, Jeff took over the company's operations, and after his death in 1927, Ben, who was already working in the industry, assumed the reins. Joe, the writer of the article above, would later jointly venture with his brother-in-law, Dr. Marcus Mashburn, to establish his own cotton seed company, the Sawnee Valley Seed Company in

Cumming, Georgia, who also marketed Summerour Half and Half Cotton.[44]

Soon the use of Homer's cotton variety ran its course. But Ben, a graduate of Georgia Tech and an astute businessman himself, would develop his own variety of cotton, marketing it under the Summerour Seed Company located in Norcross. He also continued to farm and process cotton on his farm in Warsaw. His methodology involved providing his variety of cotton seed to farmers under a contract stipulating that they follow certain guidelines, including having their cotton ginned at his own gin, at which time they would be paid for their efforts. He captured enough seed to return to the farmers in the spring and then bagged and sold the excess seed around the country. His process was so novel and so far ahead of its time that it caught the attention of the Revenue Commissioner of the State of Georgia, who sued the Summerour Seed Company in 1958. The state's contention was that the farmers were employees and thus subject to the employment laws of the state. Ben's response to the court was in the form of a letter to the judge in which he produced his contract showing that his associated farmers were contractors and not employees. He won the case and the appeal that followed.

Prior to this he'd been forced to defend his business in other ways, as shown in an article in the *Lubbock Morning Avalanche* on April 27, 1937, which detailed a federal case against a company there involving infringement on a trade name and unfair competition.[45] Following this action, Ben took out a paid advertisement in the same newspaper on May 1, 1937, with the headline, "Attention Farmers," advising the public of fake seed being marketed which was not Half and Half yet was being advertised as such. Ben was obviously intent on protecting his innovation, which had become so popular that it brought on imitators—a high compliment, to be sure.

Ben would continue to operate his seed business until the late 1950s. In January 1964 he sold the 600 acres bordering the Chattahoochee River to the Atlanta Athletic Club, which was the home club of legendary golfer Bobby Jones. The sale, as outlined in an *Atlanta Constitution* article by John Crown, mentions that the 600-acre tract was part of the Summerour family farms which included 2,117 total acres.[46] The Atlanta Athletic Club would go on to develop this as its home, hosting both the U.S. Open and PGA golf tournaments.[47]

The Summerour farms hold a rich history of Harrison's seven sons, six of whom lived long and meaningful lives. As noted earlier, two of the sons, who were also involved in farming, moved out of state: Milton Harrison lived most of his life in Mississippi, and Henry Harrison moved to Texas, where he lived out the rest of his days. The remaining brother, Thomas Edward (Tom or Tom Ed), lived his life in the area around Norcross, Georgia. After the death of his first wife, he married Margaret Eulalia (Lala) Simpson of Norcross, who was a teacher there for many years.

Lala Summerour has become the answer to one of the most oft-asked questions of those of us in Gwinnett County, Georgia: "Who is Summerour Middle School named after?" Lala did, in fact, donate a large tract of land on Mitchell Street in Norcross to be the home to both the old Norcross High School (later demolished) and Summerour Middle School, which has had two homes on the site. Lala obviously had a great love for education and for her hometown, but she did not live long enough to see the finished structure for which she is named. Still, Summerour Middle School stands there today, and a small park— Summerour Park—is located on the grounds as well.

As for the Summerour farms, they were certainly impactful in their day, as they provided a place for this generation and others who came after to make a living through farming and other related occupations. However, as time moved ahead in the 1950s, farming as a viable method of sustaining the ownership and use as agricultural land became increasingly difficult, and the land would become too valuable to continue as farmland. For those involved in this transition, it meant not only ceasing farming at some point but would result in them seeking other vocations—a transition which would span several generations and change the future of many a family.

As for the real estate itself, developers had no problem finding uses for the land which would soon. become the site of many homes, businesses, churches, and more that currently serve the Johns Creek community. Hopefully, this recounting of its origins and people will be meaningful to all who live and work there, thereby paying homage to the original Summerour families who occupied the property.

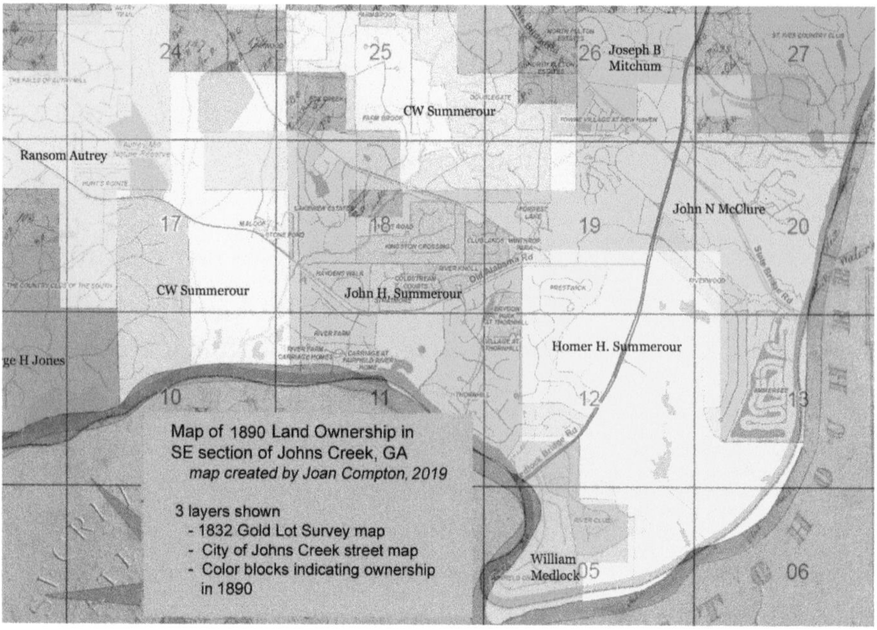

Summerour Farms Acreage, 1883

Johns Creek
CROSSING OVER
JOHNS
CREEK

Jan: 1964

$420,000 Deal

ATHLETIC CLUB TO BUY 600-ACRE TRACT HERE

By JOHN CROWN

Atlanta Journal Real Estate Editor

The Atlanta Athletic Club has voted to exercise its option to purchase for approximately $420,000 a tract in north Fulton County, The Atlanta Journal learned Tuesday. The tract is 600 acres.

The tract is one of three parcels totaling 2,117 acres owned by the Summerour family, which recently placed them on the market. Total sale price for the combined three pieces of property is about $1,172,325, Scott Hudgens Realty and Mortgage, Inc., reported. Mr. Hudgens, together with Sterling "Red" Eaves of his firm, has represented the Summerour family in the transactions.

"This represents one of the largest property turnovers in Fulton County," Mr. Hudgens declared.

THE SITE selected by the athletic club is owned by Ben Summerour. It borders the Chattahoochee River and is north of Norcross.

H. C. Allen Jr., president of the club, was reported out of town Tuesday and, therefore, not available for comment on the action, which took place Monday night.

"Mr. Allen said Monday night that insofar as we know we will exercise the option and purchase the property," Clyde Mingledorff, a club official, said. "Mr. Allen will probably appoint a committee about Jan. 1. Its job will be to consider long-range plans and make recommendations about what should be done."

Mr. Mingledorff emphasized that the north Fulton site would in no way affect the East Lake Country Club.

"Mr. Allen said he expected the East Lake club to continue to be improved,' Mr. Mingledorff commented. "He said, if for nothing else, it should be used as a shrine to golf."

Athletic Club article

Harrison Monument

John Henry Monument

Chapter 6

C. A. Summerour & Sons

Generations 6, 7

The accumulation of gold had made the Summerour family wealthy, and in the late 1800s they turned the gold into real estate—a commodity which would serve as productive family farms into the sixth, seventh, and eighth generations of the writer's family. While the real estate would one day become too valuable for farm use, at the time it provided a living for each of the large families.

John Henry died in 1903 at the age of 53, and his wife, Catherine, died in 1906, leaving their farm to their boys, including Charles Anderson (Charlie), my grandfather. Charlie had been born in the "old brick house" in 1875, just after the family moved there. Charlie had moved to Duluth before his parents' deaths and started his own family. On November 11, 1901, he married Annie Lewis, the daughter of Dr. Crawford Lewis, a physician and Civil War veteran.

While raising their young family in Duluth, Charlie likely continued his ties to the farm but also turned his interest toward other businesses. He began a retail store, Lewis and Summerour, which sold general merchandise, and he also owned a cotton gin, which kept his ties to farming. Sometime in the 1920s he moved the family back to Warsaw, where they lived in the brick homeplace, and the boys began working on the farm, where they raised cattle and chickens as well as growing crops, including cotton. The farm included two tenant houses, several barns, and chicken houses.

While farming continued to be their primary source of income, Charlie must have at some time developed a concern about the future of farming, as he later expressed the sentiment in a letter to his older brother Harrison, who had moved to Mississippi, that he "wanted to get the boys off the farm." It took several decades but was a decision that would affect all the generations that followed.

As part of his plan, Charlie, with the help of his sons, began a tannery in 1934 on what is now Abbotts Bridge Road in Duluth. The winding stretch of road soon became known as the "tannery curves"—where many speeders would meet their demise. The tannery's first structure was a barn-like wooden building along a creek, which provided the water to process the cattle hides that were soaked in concrete vats.

Finishing the leather was done with large presses that eventually made the leather into workable sides of leather. Likely, much of their original design was patterned after a long-established tannery, Bona Allen and Company, that was located about 15 miles away in Buford, Georgia.

While continuing to work the farm several miles away, the brothers soon began to manufacture leather products, which quickly became a full-scale manufacturing business. The shop building was built as a rectangle and looked a great deal like the chicken houses on the farm. It had a long shaft down the center, driven by an electric motor, which powered the various riveting, sewing, and other machinery used to process leather to make harnesses, bridles, halters, dog collars, and many other items. The business hired manufacturers' representatives to sell their products to hardware stores and feed and seed stores all over the southeast. Originally, some of my uncles actually traveled and showed samples to the stores, expanding the tannery's customer base. Later, they would develop lines of pet and horse supplies and soon developed a catalog that brought in mail orders as well.

Since I was the only nephew who lived locally, my uncles were a big part of my upbringing, and they allowed me to tag along with them. Some of my earliest memoires involve daily trips to the shop as well as the farm, where, although I was exposed to farming, the practice had begun to dwindle, and over time the farm primarily became a tenant farm.

My father was active in all phases of manufacturing, including cutting and sewing, as well as being in charge of maintaining equipment and machinery at the shop and the farm. My uncles who worked in the business were not married at the time, which led to my mother being the bookkeeper. Since I was around so much, my father eventually allowed me to try my hand at some of the processes, although my usual summer job was unloading trucks and running errands. My work on the farms was primarily limited to bailing and hauling hay, which was enough to teach me that farming was probably not in my future.

In retrospect, the lives of most of my grandfather's related family in Duluth also changed as well. His brother Frank Summerour (1884–1957) was a partner in the first funeral home in town. Cousin James Heard Summerour (1888–1950) and his son Joseph Heard Summerour Sr. (1916–1980) both served as postmaster in Duluth for over 50 years.

While change is not always positive in every respect, times had changed for the good for the most part. Life for me and my contemporaries proved that the decisions made by our ancestors were certainly positive, and our lives and futures were better because of their foresight.

C.A.Summerour

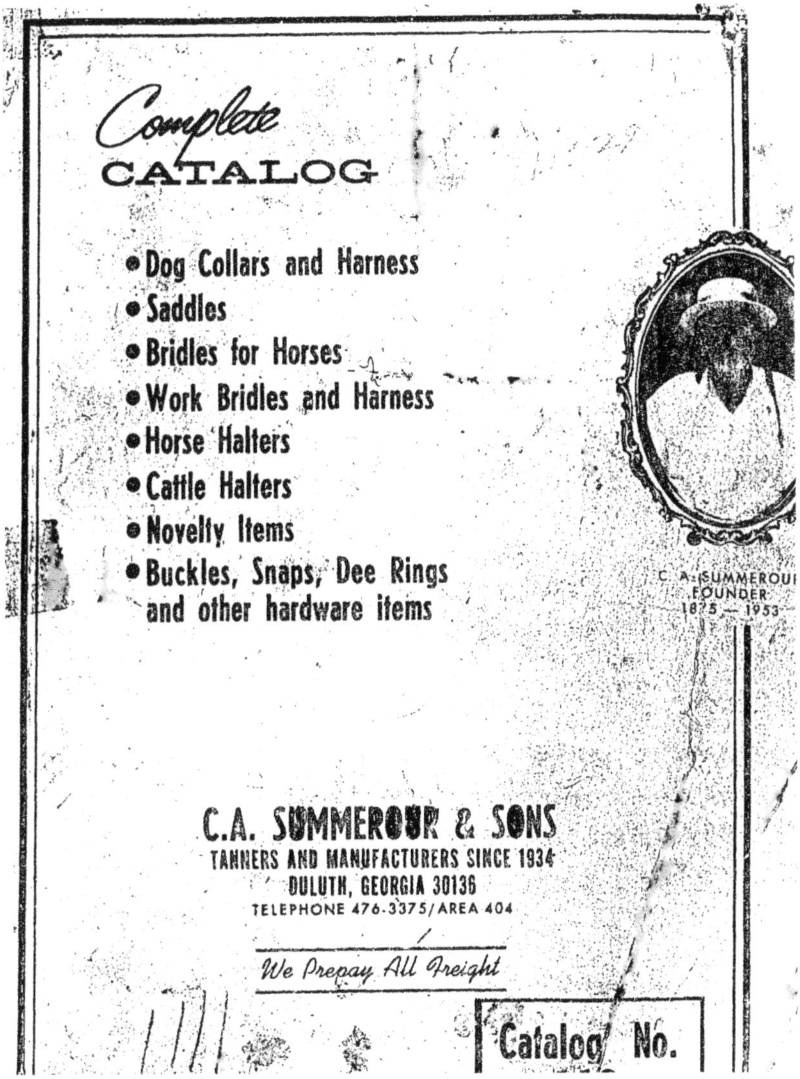
Complete
CATALOG
Dog Collars and Harness
Saddles
Bridles for Horses
Work Bridles and Harness
Horse Halters
Cattle Halters
Novelty Items
Buckles, Snaps, Dee Rings
and other hardware items
C. A. SUMMEROUR
FOUNDER
C.A. SUMMEROUR & SONS
TANNERS AND MANUFACTURERS SINCE 1934
DULUTH, GEORGIA 30136
TELEPHONE 476-3375/AREA 404
We Prepay All Freight
Catalog No.

C. A. S. Summerour Catalog

Chapter 7

Today

Generations 7, 8, 9, 10

Truly, the lifestyle as the Summerour family had experienced had gone through a major change that would impact the lives and future of my immediate family over the generations. We had more opportunity for education and a broad choice of vocations—all of which were seemingly natural to those of us who grew up in a non-agrarian setting. Our family was given these new opportunities, and my two sisters and I were able to avail ourselves of all the best of life—living in a small town, having good schools and friends, and living the American dream of our ancestors—even if we could not see the present in light of the wonderful time in which we lived.

My parents, Knox Summerour (1914–1969) and Georgia Rudene Bagwell (1917–1990), both grew up and went to school in Duluth, Georgia, including the time my father spent in Warsaw on the farm. Even though he was three years older than my mother, they graduated from high school one year apart, in 1933 and 1934, respectively. Daddy always said he was behind because he had to work on the farm, which was common for males at that time. They married and, like many young families of the day, lived with my father's family for their first few years together. My oldest sister, Gertrude, was born in 1938, and we were always told she was not given a middle name because the combination of her first and last names was already enough. Fittingly, her name was later shortened to Trudy. My other sister, Georgia "Sue," was born in 1942.

Shortly before I came along in 1948, my father obtained some family property near his homeplace, including the house where we grew up. After several renovations, central heat and air conditioning replaced the old coal stove. This house would stay in the family for many years and is located next door to where my family currently lives. Even though it is no longer owned by my immediate family, its presence there is a daily reminder of my years of upbringing, including rambling in the woods and the surrounding area. Although this area would now be considered "city living," in my childhood we had many farm animals, including chickens, cattle, and pigs. We often killed chickens for dinner, and our annual hog killings produced meat which was then stored in a small outbuilding. Later, my father also constructed a barn, which I tore down in 1977 to build our current home. To this day the entire property is terraced, as it would have been in the early farming days.

First and foremost, my father was a hard worker, whether it was working on a hay baler at the farm, on machinery at the tannery business, or at home. But he still took time to instill in me many qualities and skills—although some of his mechanical talents did not show up in me. He also loved sports, particularly, baseball, and he spent countless hours teaching me to play just as he did—throwing right-handed and hitting left-handed, a quirk that has inexplicably been passed down to two of my otherwise right-handed grandsons. While I was aware that my father loved and played sandlot baseball, only recently did I come across a photograph of him with the 1932 Duluth High School football team, taken long before the official start of football at DHS.

Later, in 1959, he would play a large part in inaugurating the first "official" high school football team in Duluth. He also helped construct the local baseball diamond where DHS now plays their home baseball games.

Sadly, my father began having heart issues at age 49, at a time when medical science had not yet advanced to the point that they could extend his life. To my great sorrow, he died in 1969 at age 55. My primary regret is that he did not live to see his grandchildren or great-grandchildren, as I know how much he would have loved to be able to interact and share his love with them. But he set high standards for hard work and integrity, which he had no doubt adopted from his ancestors, as detailed in preceding chapters.

All of my childhood took place during a time of transition from an agrarian background to other types of vocations—a hallmark of my life that was dramatically different from the previous generations. This was just as my grandfather intended.

My maternal grandmother, Pearl Bagwell, was a wonderful person who loved her family and her garden, which she worked until she was no longer physically able. She lived only a short distance away from me for several years, but after she moved next door, I was able to see her often, as she worked in the garden almost every day. She was the spiritual head of our family, always active in the Baptist Church and a writer of materials for both teachers and children. I was happy that she lived to see me ordained as a deacon in the same church, which she loved. We were blessed to have her around for a long life, as she lived until the age of 95.

My mother was primarily a homemaker, raising the three of us, but as noted earlier, she also worked at the tannery as a bookkeeper for many years. She always took care of us and made sure we had the best she could provide. When it came to school and sports, she supported my sisters as cheerleaders and never missed a basketball, football, or baseball game of mine. She loved that after marrying we were able to build our home next to her and live close to her. She was widowed for over 30 years and always told me how much she missed my father, which was a constant concern of mine after his death just prior to my finishing college. Luckily, sine we lived only a few feet from her, we were able to see her daily and help her with any needs she had. She died in 1990 at the age of 72, having lived longer than any in our immediate family. While she was able to enjoy her grandchildren in their early years, she missed the joy she would have had seeing them grow into the wonderful adults they have become.

Both of my sisters were loving people and very caring to their younger brother, who was always mingling with them and their many friends who frequented our house. My sisters had a lot in common, as both were excellent students and high scholastic achievers. When I entered first grade, we were all in the same school building, which meant it was sometimes necessary for Trudy to come and pick up her baby brother during the school day when the teacher could not stop him from crying. In high school they were both cheerleaders for the basketball team, which meant the whole family—including little brother—tagged along to games, which likely fueled my love for sports. Trudy became the first to go to college, which was exciting for the whole family. Although Trudy and Sue initially went to different small colleges, both sisters ended up at Georgia Southern College (now Georgia Southern University) in Statesboro, Georgia, which made for a long trip, considering there were no interstate highways at the time. Nonetheless, we made that trip often, which was an adventure for me. Six years apart, both Trudy and Sue graduated with degrees in education, and both had short careers in the teaching profession.

Trudy also worked in a local doctor's office, while Sue spent over 25 years as a social worker. One of the most unusual times of my life was when Trudy joined the faculty at my elementary school and became my sixth-grade teacher. While this was a novel experience, it lacked any requisite fanfare since most of my fellow students didn't seem to think I got any special treatment—and they were right! This contrasts with just a few years earlier when, as a sobbing first grader, I certainly needed her help.

Some of the most vivid memories of my youth revolve around my sister Sue's health. She was plagued by scoliosis from an early age, which meant wearing an ugly back brace and frequent visits to the doctor. She and our family became very familiar with Scottish Rite Hospital in Decatur, Georgia, where she was one of the earliest patients with that malady to undergo surgery. She required a body cast and hospital stays for months at a time. Even though this meant trips every Sunday afternoon to visit her, I was always glad to go along since it meant I got to play outside with other kids (child visitors weren't allowed in the hospital). During one hospital stay, Sue made it known that she wanted a horse after she got out, a wish our father was determined to grant. She was only able to ride the horse a few times, but even that boosted her spirits—although, in all honesty, my father sold the horse only after *he* was bucked off!

Most of what I remember about Sue and her health is her refusal to complain. Even later in life, when she was mostly housebound and not able to get out much, she seldom commented on her plight. After our mother died in 1990, Sue and her husband, Johnny Foley, moved into the home where we grew up; thus, we lived next door to Sue until her death in 2009. They had no children, but she was ever a great lover of animals, including more cats than we could ever count.

Trudy was very active in the community and at church. She married soon after college but divorced a few years later. She then married Gene Johnson, and they had one adopted son, John Charles. She was always there for me, and I knew that I could always talk to her about anything, which led to some long conversations. In this way I like to think I was able to help her after she was diagnosed with Lou Gehrig's disease in her early 60s. But the reality is that she lived her faith to the end, which was difficult, as she suffered greatly from this terrible disease now known as ALS. Thankfully, I was able to be at her side when she died in November 2002. Somewhat like her sister, Sue's determination and faith served her well in her last days on earth, and I am greatly assured that one day all three of us will celebrate life together again.

Earlier, I referenced our connection to the Knox family, whose ties to our community go back even farther than those of the Summerour family. When I was in first grade, I met Rachel Annette Knox (born in 1948) for the first time, and although we didn't date until much later in high school, we have now been married for nearly 50 years (and together for nearly 56, including our time in high school and college). She is my rock and best friend and a magnificent mother and grandmother. We attended the University of Georgia (UGA) together, and she was the first in her family to graduate from college. After graduating, she spent a short stint as a high school teacher before becoming a mom and expert homemaker. The time she spent with our three children was a blessing no amount of money could buy. After the nest was empty, she and a few of her best friends launched a successful and popular special events facility in downtown Duluth called the Payne-Corley House, which was later transitioned to our oldest daughter and her husband, who now own and manage it. Annette is known throughout town as someone who cares more about others than herself, and this is evident every day of her life.

The Summerour–Knox connection has always been somewhat of a novelty and is in some respects the product of having lived in a small community for such a long time. As noted, my father was named after the Knox family and my wife's maiden name is Knox. We compounded the situation by naming our own son Charles Knox. To add further confusion, we now live on Knox Drive, named as such to honor both the Knox family and my father, as well as John Knox, my wife's great uncle who built the first house on the property. Such things happen when your family sticks around a small town for decades; you get to name your own street and pass on your family names to your children.

As most of us know, having children brings immense change to one's life. When it happens it seems quite drastic, but later, the real joys of life begin, as do one's lasting experiences. Our first daughter, Krista Leigh (born in 1973), brought that first measure of real change to our lives. Krista has always been a high achiever, a trait which has made her a success in the business world. As mentioned previously, she and her husband, Executive Chef Michael Ganley, have parlayed their corporate experience into owning and managing the local, special events house known as the Payne-Corley House in Duluth, which has won several *Best of Gwinnett* and *Best of The Knot* awards since opening in 1999. They are both also very active in the civic and cultural life of Duluth as well as their church, which, coincidentally or not, sits on the former Summerour farm property in the aforementioned Johns Creek. But as any grandparent would say, Krista and Michael's most meaningful work was producing three fine sons: Colin Bernard (born in 2004), and twins Alex Brien and Ryan Knox (born in 2008), all of whom are true boys who love sports and adventure. As they live close by, we are fortunate to be able to spend much quality time with them.

Our second daughter, Kerri Anne (born in 1976), was a Bicentennial baby and has always been a supremely joy-filled, pleasant, and loving person. She is a devoted wife to her husband, Jeff Palm, and a remarkable mother to her two baseball-loving boys, Addison Jeffrey (born in 2004) and Jacob Charles (born in 2008). Both of them, like myself and my father before me, just so happen to throw right-handed and hit left-handed. Luckily, their ages and that of their male cousins correspond perfectly, making for fast playmates. Having five grandsons has been great for a sports-minded grandfather like me, particularly since my wife and I share a love for baseball; we have traveled all over Georgia and as far as Cooperstown, New York, and Miami, Florida, to watch them play.

As with all fathers who love sports, I longed to have a boy, and Charles Knox was born in 1980. I cherish the time we spent on baseball and basketball, as I was often his coach—although he might not have enjoyed that quite as much as I did. Later, after he developed a significant talent in music, I was relieved to hear that he did not regret all that time spent in athletics. In high school Knox became a first-class trumpet player and rose to be the #1-ranked trumpet player in Georgia in 1998 as well as first trumpet in the Atlanta Symphony Youth Orchestra (1997–98). He received a music scholarship to UGA, where he studied with well-known Canadian Brass trumpeter Fred Mills and played in the Redcoat Marching Band. After two years in Athens, he transferred to Berklee College of Music in Boston, where he finished his degree, studying film scoring. He was then invited back to UGA for a graduate assistantship where he again studied under Fred Mills, becoming close to him as a protégé and friend and obtaining a master's degree in the process. Since 2007 Knox has lived in Los Angeles, where he has worked as a film and TV composer and recorded and performed on many productions, including *American Idol* and *The Voice*. However, his best accomplishment so far has been as father to our only granddaughter, Scarlette Mae Summerour (born in 2011), whom he adores and to whom he and her mother have passed down their love of music, virtually assuring that she will be heard from in future generations. More Summerour gold found in California.

While Knox may be remembered for other accomplishments, his editing of this book and his love shown for me and my efforts make me even more thankful for him. And somewhere along the way he inherited the family trait of loyalty and faithfulness. His character and strong convictions mean a great deal to me, and I am confident these will serve him well as he moves through life.

Making commentary on my own family has been the most difficult part of writing this history, as my pride in them is indescribable. But I do not want to imply that their history is complete. I know they all have the spiritual strength and character to grow far beyond where they are now. And while I have been quite brief in describing them, my love for them and my wishes for their future are boundless. I know they will be able to achieve things others will someday chronicle, and I hope that learning their family's ancestry will help them realize they have a great heritage to extend for themselves and for their own progeny.

Knox monument

C.A. and Anne on their wedding day in 1903

Chapter 8

Last but not Final

All Generations

While this may be the last chapter of this writing, the final episode in the history of the Summerour family has not yet been recorded. If you are a Summerour by blood or by marriage—or if you are simply interested in our family—my ultimate hope is that you will build upon what you find here, further your own research, and record the history of your particular tree branch. While you are free to use my work as a basis—as I have done with the research of those before me—just know there may perchance be some inadvertent inaccuracies within it; such is the nature and the excitement of transcribing the events and personal details of one's forebears. This is part of what makes for a unique and original work, which I pray you have found this to be. Having heard from all 10 generations of this Summerour family, I trust you now have a greater appreciation of the history of these wonderful and bountifully blessed people.

Many people recount family history with the expectation they will eventually uncover "horse thieves" or worse somewhere along the way. While these 10 Summerour generations were far from perfect, it must be said that they were an upstanding and honorable people who cared for their families and their neighbors and were generous with their hard-earned wealth. What I found obvious in my search for family traits was that they truly did work hard, with honesty and compassion. Even when they may have fallen short, they tended to respond with dignify and forthrightness.

Based on their characteristic consideration for their fellow man, and considering evidence from the few obituary summaries I could get my hands on, they acted with great consideration for the unfortunate, no matter what their status in life. Regrettably, since we have so little written of the details on which we may base an assessment of their moral fiber, we are left with only these short tidbits from which to draw such conclusions—but at least we have these.

We need to remember history, learn from it, and most importantly, record it for others to read. This is the only effective way to teach others about the real attributes of their ancestors. No scribing of family history is ever completely comprehensive, but I trust this effort will help others in their knowledge and, if possible, act as a foundation on which they can build their memories in the future.

I have often alluded to the work of Ben F. Summerour (1891–1982), who did take the time and make the effort to record Summerour family history as he knew it in 1965. He closed his rendition of our lineage (to that point) by referring to another method of displaying our linage, as found in the Gospel of Luke, chapter 3, beginning with verse 23 in the King James Version of the Bible.

As Ben wished, below I am adding my name into this rendering of my family's legacy so as to honor all Summerour family members—and, especially, those in my ancestry noted here:

Charles, that was the son of Knox, that was the son of Charlie, that was the son of John, that was the son of Harrison, that was the son of Henry, that was the son of Henry, that was the son of Heinrich, that was the son of (unknown parentage back to the time of the flood), which was the son of Noah, which was the son of Lamech, that was the son of Methusala, that was the son of Enoch, that was the son of Jared, that was the son of Malalel, that was the son of Cainan, that was the son of Seth, that was the son of Adam, that was the son of God.

Descendants of Heinrich Summerour

Generation No. 1

HEINRICH[1] SUMMEROUR was born 1722 in Germany and died 1794 in Lincoln County, NC. He married MARY About 1749 in Pennsylvania.

Children of HEINRICH SUMMEROUR and MARY are:

i. **HENRY[2] SUMMEROUR II**, b. 1759, Lincoln County, NC; d. 1836, Lincoln County, NC.

ii. MICHAEL SUMMEROUR, b. 1760, Lincoln County, NC; d. 1835, Lincoln County, NC.

∞

Generation No. 2

1. **HENRY[2] SUMMEROUR II** (Heinrich[1]) was born 1759 in Lincoln County, NC, and died 1836 in Lincoln County, NC. He married ELIZABETH WEIDNER.

Children of HENRY SUMMEROUR and ELIZABETH WEIDNER are:

i. JOHN SUMMEROUR SR., b. 1791, Lincoln County, NC; d. 1867, Walton County, GA; m. MARGARET "PEGGY" BERRY.

ii. **HENRY³ SUMMEROUR III**, b. September 12, 1786, Lincoln County, NC; d. July 31, 1849, Aurora, Lumpkin County, GA.

iii. ELIZABETH SUMMEROUR, b. August 03, 1801, Lincoln County, NC; d. July 13, 1861, Lincoln County, NC.

iv. BARBARA SUMMEROUR, b. May 10, 1799, Lincoln County, NC; d. October 01, 1874, Lincoln County, NC; m. WILEY HALLMAN, March 25, 1823, Lincoln County, NC.

v. DANIEL SUMMEROUR, b. December 28, 1787, Lincoln County, NC; d. March 15, 1855, Lincoln County, NC; m. ELIZABETH GILBERT, February 12, 1809, Lincoln County, NC.

iv. CATHERINE SUMMEROUR, b. September 03, 1789, Lincoln County, NC; d. July 23, 1864, Catawba County, NC; m. DANIEL TAPSTER /FINGER, January 28, 1809, Lincoln County, NC.

v. MARY SUMMEROUR, b. September 30, 1792, Lincoln County, NC; d. May 13, 1873, Lincoln County, NC; m. (1) DAVID FINGER; m. (2) DANIEL SHRUM; 111. (3) DAVID FINGER, February 09, 1813.

vi. JACOB TAPSTER SUMMEROUR, b. February 16, 1801, Lincoln County, NC; d. June 07, 1880, Lincoln County, NC; m. BARBARA HALLMAN, March 17, 1821, Lincoln County, NC.

vii.ANNA SUMMEROUR. 1805, Lincoln County, NC; d. 1894, Lincoln County, NC; 111. LEWIS KEENER.

viii. SUSAN SUMMEROUR, b. 1806, Lincoln County,

NC; d. 1840, Lincoln County, NC; m. JONAS FINGER, April 26, 1818.

ix. SALLY SUMMEROUR, b. Unknown.

∞

2. MICHAEL[2] SUMMEOUR (Heinrich[1] Summerour) was born 1760 in Lincoln County, NC, and died 1835 in Lincoln County, NC. He married CATHERINE CLINE.

Children of MICHAEL SUMMEROUR and CATHERINE CLINE are:

i. ELIZABETH SUMMEROUR, b. Unknown.

ii. SARAH SUMMEROUR, b. Unknown.

iii. PETER SUMMEROUR, b. Unknown.

iv. HENRY SUMMEROUR, b. Unknown; m. BARBARA.

v. DAVID SUMMEROUR, b. Unknown; m. SUSANNAH RUDISILL.

vi.ANDREW SUMMEROUR, b. Unknown.

vii. JOHN SUMMEROUR, b. Unknown.

viii. MICHAEL SUMMEROUR, b. Unknown.

ix. JACOB SUMMEROUR, b. Unknown.

∞

Generation No. 3

HENRY[3] SUMMEROUR III (Henry[2], Heinrich[1]) was born September 12, 1786, in Lincoln County, NC, and died July 31, 1849, in Aurora, Lumpkin County, GA. He married SARAH SALOME SEITZ July 31, 1809, in Lincoln County, NC.

Children of HENRY SUMMEROUR and SARAH SEITZ are:

i. **HARRISON[4] SUMMEROUR**, b. 1814, Lincoln County, NC; d. 1888, Warsaw, Fulton County, GA.
ii. BENJAMIN FRANKLIN SUMMEROUR, b. 1817.
iii. MICHAEL DEKALB SUMMEROUR, b. 1819.
iv. SUSANNAH SUMMEROUR, b. 1823.
v. JOHN L. SUMMEROUR, b. 1827.
vi. ANNA MARIA SUMMEROUR, b. Unknown.

∞

Generation No. 4

HARRISON[4] SUMMEROUR (Henry[3], Henry[2], Heinrich[1]) was born 1814 in Lincoln County, NC, and died in 1888 in Warsaw, Fulton County, GA. He married MARY ANN HENDERSON Unknown in Unknown.

Children of HARRISON SUMMEROUR and MARY HENDERSON are:

i. **JOHN HENRY[5] SUMMEROUR**, b. 1850, Warsaw, Fulton County, GA; d. 1903, Warsaw, Fulton County, GA.

ii. CHARLES WILLIAM SUMMEROUR, b. 1857.

iii. THOMAS ED SUMMEROUR, b. 1859.

iv. JEFFERSON DAVIS SUMMEROUR, b. 1861.

v. MARY A SUMMEROUR, b. 1863.

vi. HOMER HIGHTOWER SUMMEROUR, b. 1866.

vii. SUSIE ELIZABETH SUMMEROUR, b. 1869.

∞

Generation No. 5

JOHN HENRY[5] SUMMEROUR *(*Harrison[4], Henry[3], Henry[2], Heinrich[1]*)* was born 1850 in Warsaw, Fulton County, GA, and died 1903 in Warsaw, Fulton County, GA. He married CATHERINE HOPE.

Children of JOHN SUMMEROUR and CATHERINE HOPE are:

i. HENRY HARRISON SUMMEROUR, b. 1871.

ii. **CHARLES ANDERSON[6] SUMMEROUR**, b. 1875, Warsaw, Fulton County, GA; d. 1953, Duluth, GA.

iii. JOHN HENDERSON SUMMEROUR, b. 1877.

iv. FRANK SUMMEROUR, b. 1884.

v. PATRICK WALTER SUMMEROUR, b. 1890.

vi. GUY SUMMEROUR, b. 1893.

∞

Generation No. 6

CHARLES ANDERSON^{6} SUMMEROUR (John Henry^{5}, Harrison^{4}, Henry^{3}, Henry^{2}, Heinrich^{1}) was born in 1875 in Warsaw, Fulton County, GA, and died 1953 in Duluth, GA. He married ANNIE E. LEWIS.

Children of CHARLES SUMMEROUR and ANNIE LEWIS are:

i. LENOIR SUMMEROUR, b. 1903.

ii. SARAH KATHERINE SUMMEROUR, b. 1905.

iii. JOHN HENRY SUMMEROUR, b. 1906.

iv. CRAWFORD LEWIS SUMMEROUR, b. 1907.

v. RICHARD SUMMEROUR, b. 1909.

vi. MAXWELL SUMMEROUR, b. 1912.

vii. **KNOX^{7} SUMMEROUR**, b. 1914, Warsaw, Fulton County, GA; d. 1969, Duluth, GA.

∞

Generation No. 7

KNOX^{7} SUMMEROUR (Charles Anderson^{6}, John Henry^{5}, Harrison^{4}, Henry^{3}, Henry^{2}, Heinrich^{1}) was born 1914 in Warsaw, Fulton County, GA, and died in 1969 in Duluth, GA. He married RUDENE BAGWELL in Norcross, GA.

Children of KNOX SUMMEROUR and RUDENE BAGWELL are:

i. GERTRUDE SUMMEROUR, b. 1938, d. 2002.

ii. GEORGIA SUE SUMMEROUR, b. 1942, d. 2009.

iii. **CHARLES OBER^{8} SUMMEROUR**, b. 1948, Duluth, GA.

∞

Generation No. 8

CHARLES OBER^{8} SUMMEROUR (Knox^{7}, Charles Anderson^{6}, John Henry^{5}, Harrison Henry^{4}, HenryIII^{3}, HenryII^{2}, Heinrich^{1}) was born in 1948 in Duluth, GA. He married ANNETTE KNOX February 13 1971 I Duluth, GA

Children of CHARLES OBER and ANNETTE KNOX SUMMEROUR are:

i. KRISTA LEIGH SUMMEROUR b. September 4, 1973 in Duluth , GA, Michael Anthony, b. April 13, 1971 in Windsor, Ontarioay Married May 1, 2002 in Bali Indonesia

ii. KERRI ANNE SUMMEROUR, b. June 20, 1976 in Atlanta, GA' Jeffrey Allen Palm,. June 14, 1971. in Pa, Ohio Married . November 3, 2001 In Duluth, GA.

iii. CHARLES KNOX SUMMEROUR, b. March 6,1980 in Duluth, GA. Joanne, Wu Born P:i-He Wu in Taipei, Taiwan Married June6, 2011 in Duluth, Ga.

∞

Generation # 9

i. KRISTA LEIGH SUMMEROUR GANLEY
ii. KERRI ANNE SUMMEROUR PALM
iii. CHARLES KNOX SUMMEROUR

∞

Generation 10

Children of KRISTA SUMMEROUR GANLEY and MICHAEL GANLEY

i. COLIN BERNARD GANLEY b. July 12, 2004 in Lawrenceville GA.
ii. ALEX BRIEN GANLEY, b. September 7 2008, in Lawrenceville, GA/
iii. RYAN KNOX GANLEY b. September 7, 2008 in Lawrenceville, GA.

Children of KERRI SUMMEROUR PALM and JEFFREY PALM: b.

i. ADDISON JEFFREY PALM b. October 4, 2004 in Atlanta, GA.
ii. JACOB CHARLES PALM, b. July 16, 2008 in Atlanta, GA.

Children of KNOX SUMMEROUR and JOANNE WU SUMMEROUR

i. SCARLETTE MAE SUMMEROUR b. December 4 2011 in Huntington Beach, CA.

Bibliography

About North Georgia-Old Federal Road. www.aboutnorthgeorgia.com.

Atlanta Constitution. Obituary of Harrison Summerour. January 1888.

Atlanta Constitution. Obituary of John Henry Summerour. November 13, 1903.

Atlanta History Center, Francis C. Smith Collections. p. 201.

Bagley, Gerald C. *History of Forsyth County, Georgia.* Southern Historical Press.

Bockus, Susan. *Why Germans Came to Philadelphia.* Article 16. May. www.wnam.net.

Bridges, David, Records of the Gold Mine Museum, Dahlonega, Georgia. 1996.

Cook, Robert C. *Mines of Georgia: Their Properties and Occurrences.* State of Georgia

Department of Natural Resources. Atlanta, 1988.

Coulter, E. Merton, *Auraria–The Story of a Georgia Gold-Mining Town,* The University of Georgia Press, 1956; paperback, 2009.

Dawson County Historical Society. https://www.dawsoncounty.org/history.

Descendants of Heinrich Summerour. Maiden, North Carolina, NCGen Web Project. www.ncgenweb.us/maiden

Find A Grave. Jacob McCartney Scudder. https://www.findagrave.com.

Find A Grave. Old White Church Cemetery. https://www.findagrave.com.

Forsyth County Historical Society. Bell Research Center.

Franklin Creighton Mines. https://www.wikipedia.com.

German Settlers in the Appalachians. https://digitalheritage.org/2012/10/german-settlers-in-the-appalachians/

George Heinrich (Weidner) Whitner (1727–1792). https://www.wikitree.com.

Georgia Gold Rush. https://www.wikipeia.com.

German Settlers. https://www.ncpedia.org.

German Genealogy–Palatinate (Pfalz). https://www.familysearch.com.

Passenger List of the Ship *Patience.* www.trailofourancestors.com / shiplidy31.htm

Germany–18th Century History. https://www.wikipedia.com.

Grenke, William H. *The Beginnings of the Pennsylvania-German Element in Rowan and Cabarrus County, North Carolina.* 1984.

Gwinnett Daily News. "Cotton Developer Dies." March 9, 1982.

Huxley, Thomas, *Lay Sermons, Addresses and Reviews* (New York, Appleton, 1871), p. 20. *Henry_Weidner, His Life and Character, A Memorial Service.* Published by Hickory Printing Company, May 30, 1894.

Lawrenceville New Herald. "Once Grand Dwelling Now in Ruins." July 14, 1962.

Lubbock Morning Avalanche. "Notice Farmers!" April 28, 1957.

Lubbock Morning Avalanche. "Suit Filed Here in Seed Case." April 28, 1957. p. 1.

McGee, Thomas. Sketch of Howell Mansion. Acquired 2005.

Milton County. https://www.georgiaencyclopedia.org.

Milton Court of Ordinary Minutes, Abstract. Book C., 1894-1909.

Newton Enterprise, The. *Henry Weidner: His Life and Character,* Catawba County, North Carolina. May 30, 1894.

Owenby, Ted and David Wharton, *Georgia's Old Federal Road, Phase I.,* Submitted to the Georgia State Department of Transportation. Published by the University of Pennsylvania Press, 2007.

Passage to America, 1750. eyewitnesstohistory.com.

Reidy, Myra. *Historic Forsyth.* August 2011. www.400online.com.

Shadburn, Donald L. *Blood Kin: Pioneer Cherokees in Upper Georgia Centered In Forsyth*

County, Georgia. Self-published. January 1, 1999.

Shadburn, Donald L. *Unhallowed Intrusion: A History of Cherokee Families in Forsyth County, Georgia.* Cottonpatch Press, 1993.

Teller, Susan Moore *Eliza: A Blue Blooded Southern Belle Who Became a Pioneer Woman.* Lulu.com, October 2018.

Teller, Susan Moore *The Saxons: Story of the Summerour Family in America.* Lulu.com, January 2020.

Wells, Don and Dianne, *Thar's Gold in Them Thar Hills, pat 3,* Digital Library of Georgia, www.dig.usg.edu

Acknowledgments

So much has gone into the work of getting this book published that may not be apparent to most readers. But without the contributions of the following, nothing you have read would be possible, and I want to express my appreciation here to honor ad give recognition to these special people.

Joan Compton

Joan is the President of the Johns Creek (GA) Historical Society and has embraced the many challenges of making the residents of this young city aware of their history. In the process, she developed a love and knowledge of the Summerour family, and she gladly allowed me to use her work here. Just as important was her support and encouragement along the way. She is a special person who loves and appreciates history. It is only fitting that she lives on a portion of the Summerour family land where I spent so much time growing up.

April Fields

April has been involved in numerous aspects of publishing for over 35 years. She has become known as a mentor in helping struggling authors find a route to publication, and she provided direction and guidance to me for which I am very appreciative. She lives with her family in Buford, Georgia, and really enjoys her time on her boat at Lake Lanier.

Lisa M. Russell

Lisa is a writing instructor and assistant academic dean. She loves to write micro-histories and has published books such as *Lost Towns of North Georgia* and *Underwater Ghost Towns.* She is very active in local Georgia historical societies and has been a wonderful mentor to me, providing much guidance and inspiration in my publishing journey.

Donald L. Shadburn

Don was a gifted writer and researcher who published much of the history of his native Forsyth County, Georgia. His special interest is in the history of the Cherokee Nation, particularly as it related to the mixed blood families, which led him to write some of the most detailed books on this subject. His numerous books include *Cherokee Planters in Georgia,* and *Unallowed Intrusion: A History of Cherokee Families in Forsyth County, Georgia.* I was honored to know Don and have him give me an autographed a copy of *Unhallowed Intrusion* shortly before his death in 2010. His books noted here were often referenced and quoted and were extremely beneficial to me. My only regret is that I did not meet him earlier, as his work will always be with us.

Ben F. Summerour

Cousin Ben, as my father referred to him, published the first family history that I first saw and I was captivated by its detail and thoroughness—all done from his personal memory and contacts with other trusted family sources. His family tree and stories about key family members became my primary point of reference, and I have used it many times to verify and document my work. *A Statement and/or Survey of the Summerour Family* has been copied and circulated to many family members and served as an inspiration to me of how important it is to document our family history.

Ethel and Florence Summerour

Ethel and Florence are sisters who grew up in Lucedale, MS. They spent much of their 90 years gathering, compiling, and documenting much of their Summerour ancestry. By the time I met them in 1980, they had accumulated a large notebook that covered every branch of our family. They were kind enough to share all that they had—which had been accumulated by phone and mail—with me. It has always been treasured and is referenced in my work.

Susan Teller Moore

Susan is first a family member but is also a gifted author, publisher, genealogist, and long-time member of the Daughters of the America Revolution. She recently authenticated our common ancestor, Henry Summerour III, as a patriot, for which she received special recognition from the DAR. Among her writings are two publications about her Summerour ancestry—*Eliza: A Southern Belle Who Became a Pioneer Woman* and *The Saxons: Story of the Summerour Family in America.* She provided substantial and much appreciated support in my work. For many years she has administered a family site on Facebook—Descendants of Heinrich Summerour—which has helped many family members stay in touch with their ancestors.

Earlayne Chance

As one of the longest term family researchers, Earlayne has been an inspiration and source of much family history. She is a descendant of Michael Summerow (161-1835), son of Henirich Summerour (1715-1792) and brother of my direct descendant Henry Summerour (1769-1836) Over 20 years ago I was able to help her with a DNA test which helped prove this connection despite the differing spelling of the surname. The test also documented my direct connection to Heinrich Summerour. Earlayn is an accomplished artist and now lives in Ruidoso, NM.

Special Thanks to

Biff and Nancy Barnes, Stories To Tell Books

Endnotes

1 E. Merton Coulter, *Auraria, The Story of A Georgia Gold-Mining Town*, University of Georgia Press, 1956, Paperback, 2009, p. 2.

2 Coulter, E. Merton, *Auraria*, p. 8

3 The Western Herald, cited by E. Merton Coulter, in *Auraria, A Georgia Gold-Mining Town*, p. 9.

4 Coulter, E. Merton, *Auraria*, p. 11.

5 Benjamin F. Summerour, A Statement and/or Survey Covering the Summerour Family. Self-published 1965.
6 Ibid

7 Don and Diane Wells, Thars Gold in Them There Hills, The Georgia Digital Library. *www.Dgl.usg.edu.*

8 Obituary of David Allen Summerour, Clipping from unknown newspaper.

9 *Ancestors of Susan Rebekkah W. Sloan*, from Susann Moore Teller. Self-published family history.

10 Ancestry.com

11 Wikipedia; Wikipedia.com.; 2020

12 German Settlement in Pennsylvania;; www.hsp.org; 2020.

13 Ibid., p. 2. .

14 Ibid.

15 Wiilliam H. Grehnke; *The Beginnings of the Pennsylvania-German Element in Rowan and Cabarrus Counties, North Carolina*; University of Pennsylvania Press; Vol. 58, No. 4 (1954), p. 1. www.jstor.org.

16 Donna Spence Rhinehart, On Search of Our Ancestors. Genealogy, The Patience, www.searchofourancestors, 2019

17 The Newton Enterprise, courtesy of Susan Moore Teller. "The Story of the Saxon, Henry of Wetin, Coburg, Germany, the Pioneers Summerour Family in the Founding of America," published 2020.

18 A Statement or Survey Covering the Summerour Family; Ben F. Summerour, 1965; Self-published.

19 Ted Ownby and David Wharton, *Georgia's Old Federal Road*, University of Mississippi; 2015, p. 2.

20 Ibid. .

21 Don Shadburn; *Unhallowed Intrusion, A History of Cherokee Families in Forsyth County, Georgia* Published by The Cotton Patch Press, p. 316.

22 Shadburn, *Unallowed Intrusion, A History of Cherokee Families in Forsyth County, Georgia*; p. 317.

23 Ibid., 487.

24 Ibid., 529

25 Ibid., p. 520.

26 Ibid., p.535.

27 Ibid., p. 34.

28 Ibid., p.45.

29 Ibid., p. 672, Appendices.

30 Historic Forsyth by Myra Reidy, www.400online.com, August 2011.

31 "Dawson County History," www. dawsoncounty.org., 2013

32 Ibid.

33 The *Forsyth County News*, "History of Half-and Half Cotton," Joseph Summerour. April 1949.

34 *Atlanta Constitution*, January 18, 188; www.newspapers.com

35 www.In2013dollars.com/us/inflation. 1860; 2020

36 The *News Herald*, Lawrenceville, GA. Thursday, July 18, 1963.

37 Ben F. Summerour, A Statement and/or Survey Concerning the Summerour Family, self-published, December 1965

38 *Atlanta Constitution*, November 15, 1903

39 www.johnscreekga.gov, 2020.

40 Thomas Huxley, Lay Sermons, Addresses and Reviews.

41 Joseph Edwin Summerour, "History of Half and Half Cotton," Forsyth County News; April 7, 1949

42 Ibid., p. 2.

43 Ibid

44 "Lubbock Morning Avalanche", April 28, 1937, p. 1. Ibid, May 1, 1937, p. 3.

45 *Atlanta Constitution*, July, 1964, by John Crown

46 John Crown, *The Atlanta Constitution*, January 1964

47 Gwinnett Public Schools, https://www.gcpsk12.org/Page/25909. 2020

CPSIA information can be obtained
at www.ICGtesting.com
Printed in the USA
BVHW022042200222
629613BV00017B/237

9 780578 958446